CISTERCIAN STUDIES SERIES: NUMBER FOUR

PRAKTIKOS

CHAPTERS ON PRAYER

CISTERCIAN STUDIES SERIES

CISTERCIAN STUDIES SERIES: NUMBER FOUR

Evagrius Ponticus

THE PRAKTIKOS
CHAPTERS ON PRAYER

Translated, with an introduction and notes, by

John Eudes Bamberger ocso

CISTERCIAN PUBLICATIONS
Spencer, Massachusetts
1970

Cistercian Studies Series: ISBN 0-87907-800-6
This volume   cloth: ISBN 0-87907-804-9
                  paper: ISBN 0-87907-904-5

Library of Congress Catalog Card Number: 76-152483

© Cistercian Publications, Inc., 1972

Spencer, Massachusetts
Roscrea, Ireland

Ecclesiastical permission to publish this book was received from
Ignace Gillet, Archabbot of Cîteaux, and Bernard Flanagan,
Bishop of Worcester, April 23, 1969.

Printed in the Republic of Ireland by
Cahill & Co. Limited, Parkgate Printing Works, Dublin

CONTENTS

ABBREVIATIONS

ACW   *Ancient Christian Writers* (Westminster, Md., 1946–)

DS   *Dictionnaire de Spiritualité* (Paris, 1932–)

DTC   *Dictionnaire de Théologie Catholique* (Paris, 1903–1950)

ES   J. Muyldermans, *Evagriana Syriaca* (Louvain, 1952)

LH   Palladius, *The Lausiac History*. ACW 34 (Washington, 1964)

LTK   *Lexikon für Theologie und Kirche*. 2 ed. (Freiburg, 1957–1966)

PG   *Patrologia Graeca*. Ed. J. P. Migne (Paris, 1844–1855)

PL   *Patrologia Latina*. Ed. J. P. Migne (Paris, 1857–1866)

OCP   *Orientalia Christiana Periodica* (Rome, 1935–)

PO   *Patrologia Orientalis*. Ed. R. Griffin, F. Nau (Paris, 1897–)

RAM   *Revue d'Ascetique et de Mystique* (Toulouse, 1920–)

RSR   *Recherches des Sciences Religieuses* (Louvain, 1912–)

SC   *Sources Chrétiennes* (Paris, 1942–)

TP   A. and C. Guillaumont, *Traité Pratique ou le Moine*, SC 170, 171 (Paris, 1971)

ZAM   *Zeitschrift für Askeze und Mystik* (Munich, 1926–)

PREFACE

AT FIRST SIGHT one is surprised to see the writings of a Greek author of the fourth century in a series of publications which go under the title of "Cistercian," that is, concerned with the monastic order founded in the Middle Ages, in the West and, although today spread out across the world from the British Isles to Japan, still not having any monasteries in the Greek Near East. However, as we shall see, these texts have a real significance for Cistercian studies. Unfortunately, up to now only patrologists or others versed in Syriac, Greek, Armenian, or Latin could have access to them. Now they are readily available in English thanks to the learning and labors of a Cistercian monk who is an orientalist, one familiar with the original languages, who has done graduate study in the field and who has published articles in reviews devoted to oriental studies. In addition, he is also a psychiatrist with considerable practical experience in monastic spirituality. Thus, he keeps in close contact with real life and ably brings to the fore Evagrius' great psychological insight.

As with all the great spiritual masters of antiquity, Evagrius offers not only interest but also something of practical value. This is true in regards to his own life but also in his being a witness to an ever-living tradition and a practical and stimulating guide for working out a way of life even today.

The writings left by Evagrius have contributed to the building of the spiritual tradition from which we all draw. During his lifetime he was criticized. After his death his writings were attacked—to a

greater or lesser extent, according to the times and the regions—
and even sometimes condemned. Sometimes he was also praised.
But more frequently he was ignored, either because certain of his
writings were attributed to others or else because the texts were lost
only to be found recently by manuscript hunters. However, in the
living currents of spirituality his influence was constantly at work,
like some underground river giving freshness and vitality to the
soil and causing springs to erupt, further and further along, where-
ever it flowed unseen, unknown. In the West those of his texts
which were of a more practical nature—particularly his sentences
which were so easy to memorize—circulated in several Latin
versions.[1] Throughout the Middle Ages they spread through
Europe from monastery to monastery in Italy, France, Austria,
Spain. An eighth-century monk of Ligugé inserted certain extracts
from his writings into a sort of digest which he entitled *Liber
Scintillarum, A Book of Sparks,* which was very widely diffused.
A Cistercian of Clairvaux in the twelfth century did much the
same.

However, to understand the role of Evagrius in the evolution of
Christian spirituality and to situate him properly in relation to the
twelfth century and in particular to the Cistercians, it is necessary
to enter more deeply into the matter. A mere historical knowledge
of the man and the diffusion of his works is not sufficient. It is
necessary to seek to grasp, as a whole, the religious experiences
which fashioned the milieu of which Evagrius was a part, and which
gave direction to the tradition which would inspire the lives of the
monks of the Middle Ages and find a reflection in their writings.
We actually know relatively little of the events of the life of
Evagrius and only some of his writings have come down to us, in

---

1. B. Lambert, "Sententiae ad coenobitas translatae a S. Hieronymo (recte
Rufino)," *Bibliotheca Hieronymiana Manuscripta* (Steenbrugge, 1970), pp.
455-7, gives the list of the manuscripts of the sentences of Evagrius according to the three Latin translations: 26 mss. of which 24 are of the seventh to
twelfth centuries, 2 of the fifteenth century. This indicates a rather large
circulation and influence of these sentences during the early Middle Ages and
the Golden Age of Cîteaux. Twenty of them certainly come from monasteries;
the six others are of unknown provernance.

some cases only in translation. But more important than this transmission of texts, it is his ideas and above all the general spiritual attitude, the "religious mentality," of which he was a witness, that have been assimilated.

Evagrius and Hellenic Christianity

Evagrius himself was but a link in tradition, the tradition which introduced into Christianity elements of Greek thought—Hellenic or Hellenistic—without however "Hellenizing" faith in Christ and life in Christ. That is to say, without reducing the Church to nothing more than a school of philosophy, without causing it to lose its specific character, the unique character which it had received from God through his revelation. We have here the phenomenon of humanism which from the very origins of Christianity has shown that, without ceasing to be herself and betraying her divine origins, the Church can integrate all that is human because she exists among men for men, men in whom God was already at work before they ever knew of the Gospel. The Second Vatican Council reasserted this principle which the Fathers of the Church had formulated and put into practice.[2]

Christianity did absorb much from the Hellenic culture. In this sense there was a "Christian Hellenism." One could say that there was a certain "Hellenization" of Christianity, however within the limits which we will indicate. This delicate problem of "Hellenization" and, by consequence, of eventual "de-Hellenization" of the different manifestations of Christian life, has been the object of many studies for quite some time now, but most especially has there been a renewal of interest in it during the past fifteen years. At first there was a tendency to denounce "Hellenization" as a corruption of Christianity. Then, and especially in more recent years, scholars have zealously devoted themselves to all the different aspects—

2. The Decree, *Ad gentes,* on the missionary activity of the Church, n. 18; Declaration, *Nostra aetate,* on the non-Christian religions, n. 2.

historical, philological, biblical, patristic—of this extremely complex problem, and now their conclusions are for the most part positive. It will suffice here to cite but one witness: "The Hellenistic tradition provided the necessary conditions of possibility for a clearer affirmation of the divinity of Jesus Christ and the universality of the eschatological self-revelation of God in the face of Jesus."[3]

Certainly the process of Hellenization had its risks. This is true of any great development within the Church or in human society. There was a danger of the contamination of the faith or of Christian practice by profane or even pagan ideas. There were abuses and deviations, but the Holy Spirit animates the Church, and under his breath those men of God who were the Fathers of the Church, above all the great bishops and doctors of the third and fourth centuries, played a double role. They conserved the Christian message in its purity and they enriched it with cultural elements coming from Hellenism. It is true that some among them on certain particular points were too influenced by the Greek milieu in which they lived. But as a whole they did not fail in their mission. The most recent study on this question ends with this conclusion: "If in many cases we must recognize the effects of language on ideas—an effect often profound and sometimes sweeping—it nevertheless remains that the thought and experience themselves are original and in the final count authentically Christian. One can adopt here, making the necessary transposition, the words of M. Harl concerning Philo: 'Apparently very Greek, profoundly very Christian.' "[4]

Evagrius and Early Oriental Monasticism

An American monk has spoken of the "de-Hellenization of monasticism,"[5] and there is certainly something to be done in that

---

3. David W. Tracy in *Catholic Biblical Quarterly*, 31 (1969), 287.
4. P. T. Camelot, "Hellénisme," DS 44–45 (1968), 164.
5. M. Ohlislager, "Dehellenization of Monastic Life," *American Benedictine Review*, 18 (1967), 517–530. Father Bamberger has formulated in relation to

direction to the extent that some elements of the monastic spirituality of today are still too marked by ideas which do not come directly from the Gospel. Yet it is necessary to look to the Fathers in order not to lose anything of the human values which monasticism has Christianized. Evagrius offers in this regard a valuable contribution.

He is inseparable from his source and his milieu. And from this point of view his texts give an introduction to the world which gave birth to Origen, Gregory of Nyssa and all the great writers who gave a doctrinal expression to the spiritual experience of thousands of anonymous ascetics. The originators of the monastic way of life—[Anthony] and the hermits, [Pachomius] and his disciples who lived in common—were not especially marked by Hellenism. But very soon there appeared the theologians who were the interpreters and guides of those who were simple practitioners. These could elaborate the "theory" because they themselves also had the "practice." Historians have sufficiently demonstrated that Evagrius depends on Origen and Gregory of Nyssa so that there is no need to insist upon it here. Let us simply underline the fact that in spite of these influences he retained his own proper character. Less biblical than his two masters, he was more philosophical. In this regard he brought about in relation to them a certain evolution, which, while not without its dangers, was a step forward. More than they, he concentrated on the questions of asceticism and prayer. It is above all in relation to prayer that he introduced ideas which have served as a ferment throughout the whole course of tradition and continue to be active in our own times. For the mystery and the practice of prayer—above all contemplative prayer—raises questions which to some seem new, but which are in fact the same which have confronted every period of Christian life when man has stood before God in that eminent attitude of soul where faith touches as it were its object, unable to grasp it yet ever reaching for it. One of

the problem treated in this article certain useful and well founded reservations in his comment on it in *Collectanea Cisterciensia,* 31 (1969), "Bulletin of Monastic Spirituality," n. 313, 338, pp. 261 and 270.

the most outstanding orientalists of our times who is at the same time a great man of the spirit, Father Irenée Hausherr, summed it up when he spoke of a work of Evagrius as the "lessons of a contemplative."[6]

As Father Bamberger has well shown, Evagrius knew by experience the inner struggles of man; he knew of all the tensions, the dissensions, the revolts, the manifestations of anarchy, the aggressiveness, the self-hatred, the hatred of God and man that every man conceals within himself. In one of his works, the *Antirrheticos*, he describes sensible and imaginative obsessions which make the temptations of St Anthony seem as the dreams of a mere infant.[7] It is necessary to interpret these hallucinations with an objective realism, in the way that one of the best scholars of early monasticism has done in regards to St Anthony.[8] Beneath all the literary form—and without doubt the humor—that is employed in the expression of the psychic phenomenon we must discern quite simply the daily efforts of a converted sinner who, though given entirely over to God, yet continues to experience the resistance of his superficial "ego" until at length from the depths there emerges his true self. That which is called today "depth psychology" does not in actual fact reach the deepest part of man where the image of God resides in him. It is this obscure presence of God in his depths that man must discover and bring to light. Then in him in a certain sense God encounters God by the spirit of the risen Christ, and then there is peace: that calm, that security, that repose, that Sabbath, that leisure, that reality so rich that it can not be circumscribed by any words. This is what the term *hesychia* said for Evagrius and his contemporaries, when it is properly understood in the context of all the other terms which are complementary to it and give greater precision to its meaning.

---

6. I. Hausherr, *Les leçons d'un contemplatif: Le Traité de l'oraison d'Evagre le Pontique* (Paris, 1960).

7. Ed. W. Frankenberg, "Evagrius Ponticus," *Abhandlungen der königlichen Gesellschaft der Wissenschaften zu Göttingen, Phil.-hist. Klasse,* N.F. XIII, 2 (Berlin, 1912): a text of the Syriac version with a facing Greek text.

8. H. Dörries, in *Wort und Stunde,* II (Göttingen, 1968), 268.

The author of the most recent complete study which has appeared on hesychasm could write that Evagrius was only "the echo of the teaching which had passed from master to disciple among the Egyptian solitaries. The *hesychia* which he recommended was solitude in silence apart from the world. But more important was solitude of the spirit . . . ('the spirit-monk') ; the intellect itself—one could say just as well the heart—became monk, interior eremitism or anchoritism. On this point also Evagrius, whatever other personal and learned theories he held in regard to contemplation, was a witness to the great hesychastic tradition."[9] And this same historian brought out that a part of the vocabulary and ideas of this tradition has been conserved in the Western monasticism of the Middle Ages. This is especially true of the Cistercian school. But in this school above all, "this hesychasm seems to have been historically much less associated than in the Orient with the properly anchoritic life. Between the hesychastic ideal and the cenobitic life there was in the West much more of a synthesis than a marked opposition. The *quies monastica* in the quest of contemplation was a reality for all the monks, something they ought to tend towards by their vocation even if they were not all hermits."[10]

Evagrius and Western Monasticism

During the course of the Latin Middle Ages, Evagrius was used. He was adapted to the new historical situation and to a mentality different from that of his original milieu. The field of application of his ideas was extended to the mental structures and institutions of the medieval West. In this sense it is possible to speak of even a "Benedictine and Cistercian Evagrius." It is necessary to consider the great steps of the process by which this took place from the

---

9. P. Adnès, "Hésychasme," DS, 44–5 (1968), 388.

10. P. Adnès, *ibid.,* col. 398–9, makes a résumé of what I have said concerning "Latin hesychasm" in *Otia monastica: Etudes sur le vocabulaire de la contemplation au moyen âge, Studia Anselmiana,* 51 (Rome, 1963).

time of Evagrius himself until the twelfth century, the Cistercian Century.

Cassian. The first step of this evolution was marked by the influence of Cassian, the writer whose *Conferences* were recommended by the *Rule* of St Benedict. In these conferences he offered an initial synthesis of the monastic experience of the Orient with the spirit of the West. This ascetic and contemplative synthesis can not be separated from a particular aspect of the teaching of John Cassian which has not always been given the attention it merits. It is what a recent historian has called the "Christological aspect."[11] Certainly this aspect was not lacking in the writings of Evagrius. But it is found there more by way of allusion than by elaboration. Evagrius could not profit by the many precisions which were required in the course of the studies and the disputes which marked the growth of the Trinitarian and Christological doctrine of the Church. It was possible for one to say that "the mysticism of Evagrius was closer to that of Buddhism than that of Christianity."[12] It was the role of Cassian on this point, as well as on others, to "purify" the teaching of Evagrius,[13] but the Christology of Cassian itself needs to be situated in a larger context and clarified by other sources.

Nevertheless it is true that in order to understand Cassian, it is necessary to know Evagrius. And because Cassian is a source of St Benedict—his *Rule* depends on him and explicitly refers to him—one must say that Evagrius forms a part of the Benedictine and Cistercian tradition. From this point of view a translation of Evagrius has its importance. It ought to aid the Cistercians of today and others also to attain to a greater understanding of early monasticism which today's monasticism ought not simply to copy but ought to look to as a source of continual inspiration.

11. V. Codina sj, *El aspecto cristologico en la espiritualidad de Juan Casiano* (Rome, 1966).

12. V. Codina, *ibid.*, p. 75, citing H. U. von Balthasar, "Metaphysik und Mystik des Evagrius Ponticus," *Zeitschrift für Aszese und Mystik,* 14 (1939), 39.

13. V. Codina, *ibid.,* 104, citing A. Guillaumont, *Les "Kephalaia Gnostica" d'Evagre le Pontique* (Paris, 1962), 334.

The Early Middle Ages. In actual fact the spiritual teaching of early Eastern monasticism has penetrated the whole of the Western Middle Ages to a degree greater than one often suspects. Here is an area for careful study which remains to be explored, and perhaps this new translation can inspire such an undertaking. Attention was especially drawn to this point in the course of the eighth centenary of St Bernard in 1953. A few years later I attempted to present the results of the studies made up to that point.[14] Quite recently a scholarly study of John Scotus Eriugena and his influence has provided new information. Lacking an overall study, which will have to be prepared by a qualified group of scholars, we can consider this particular case which exemplifies the transpositions and the continual reinterpretations which made up the teaching of the great spiritual authors of the West.

John Scotus, called Eriugena, that is to say "of Irish origin," came from that country to the Continent in the ninth century. He entered into the development of ideas which animated the Carolingian Empire and many of the monasteries of that time. He translated into Latin, sometimes with commentary, the works of three Greeks who came to have very great influence on the monastic thought of the twelfth century. There was first of all the Pseudo-Denis. His translation was "for three centuries and more the fundamental text for the study of Denis in the West."[15] But Denis was read more particularly among the scholars and in actual fact had little influence on the monastic spirituality of the Western Middle Ages. But the case was otherwise with the other two authors whom Eriugena made more commonly available. One was Maximus the Confessor whose *Ambigua* and *Quaestiones ad Thalassium* were translated into Latin by John Scotus. These texts are found among monastic manuscripts, especially in the codex of Clairvaux of the twelfth century.[16] The other witness of early

14. *The Love of Learning and the Desire for God* (New York, 1962), 94–115.

15. E. Jeauneau, *Jean Scot. Homélie sur le Prologue de Jean, Introduction* (Paris, 1969), SC 151, 28, citing H. Dondaine, *Le Corpus dionysien de l'Université de Paris au XIIIe siècle* (Rome, 1953), 28.

16. *Ibid.,* 32.

mysticism was Gregory of Nyssa whom we have seen was very close to Evagrius. To his treatise, *On the Creation of Man*, Scotus gave the title, *On the Image*.[17] The notion expressed by this word, *image*, was central in the Cistercian theology of the twelfth century, and Father Déchanet has established that William of St Thierry used the translation of Gregory of Nyssa which was prepared by Scotus.[18]

The monks were attracted by what was most "contemplative" in the work of Eriugena, his long and admirable homily on the prologue of the Fourth Gospel. It was due to this that monastic tradition came to speak of "John the Theologian," that is to say, "John the Contemplative."[19] This text is found in many manuscripts coming from Cistercian and Benedictine abbeys,[20] in particular from Cîteaux[21] and Clairvaux.[22] The homily was read at the Office in the monastery[23] and a Cistercian chronicler at the end of the twelfth century, Helinand of Froidmont, gave voice to the praise of Eriugena because of the "perspicacity of his genius and the sweetness of his language."[24]

The Twelfth-Century Cistercians. The influence exercised on St Bernard by Maximus the Confessor and Gregory of Nyssa has already been pointed out by Gilson.[25] The various studies on St

17. *Ibid.*, 34.

18. *Ibid.*, 36, referring to J. M. Déchanet, *Aux sources de la spiritualité de Guillaume de Saint-Thierry* (Bruges, 1940), and *Guillaume de Saint-Thierry. L'homme et son oeuvre* (Bruges, 1942). The latter has been published in English.

19. In *Etudes sur le vocabulaire monastique du moyen âge, Studia Anselmiana*, 48, (Rome, 1961), 74–5, 92, 151, I have cited some texts.

20. E. Jeauneau, *op. cit.*, 81–113.

21. *Ibid.*, 86.

22. See *ibid.* in the Index, 388, the list of manuscripts of Troyes coming from Clairvaux. Ms. Troyes 1234, whose origin is not indicated there, comes from Clairvaux. Cf. Harmand, *Catalogue général des manuscrits des Bibliothèques publiques des Départements*, II (Paris, 1855), 506.

23. E. Jeauneau, *op. cit.*, 131.

24. *Ibid.*, 62, n. 1, citing Hélinand, *Chronicon*, Book 46 (PL 212:870 D–871 D) and pointing out this notice of Hélinand.

25. *La théologie mystique de S. Bernard* (Paris, 1934), 39–42, 29–30.

Bernard which were published on the occasion of the eighth
centenary of his death in 1953 brought to light how much the
Abbot of Clairvaux and the other Cistercian authors of his time
looked back to Origen, to Maximus the Confessor, to Gregory of
Nyssa, to other witnesses of the Greek patristic age, to Cassian,
and to John Scotus.[26] They reproduced in some way the earlier
milieu as a whole for the Middle Ages, which were more aware of
general tendencies than detailed doctrine. Evagrius was part of
this whole. At the root of his teaching, as with all the others,
is to be found Origen, and the more one studies St Bernard the
more one is convinced that he owes a great deal to Origen.[27]
Recently John Morson has brought out how much Guerric of
Igny also owes to Origen.[28]

But rather than accumulate here a collection of detailed texts, it
is more important to point out the general lines which the whole
early tradition of Christian Platonism gave to the monastic writers
of the Middle Ages and, especially, to the Cistercian School of the
twelfth century. For it was in the development of this general
orientation that Evagrius had a decisive role. A scholar who knows
well this tradition has shown how important Evagrius was for the
formation of the anthropology of the Latin Middle Ages, that
anthropology which was expressed especially in the treatises *De
Anima* which in one form or another were left to us by all the
great Cistercian writers of the twelfth century.[29] One can say the
same for the monastic anthropology of the ninth century.[30] The

26. See "Saint Bernard théologien," *Analecta S. Ordinis Cisterciensis,* 9 (1953),
316–323, under the names which we will cite as we go along.

27. The references are indicated in the Index of J. Leclercq, *Recueil d'études
sur S. Bernard,* I (Rome, 1962), 359; II (Rome, 1966), 395; III (Rome, 1969), 429.

28. J. Morson, "Guerric d'Igny," DS, 6 (1967), 1118.

29. Endre von Ivánka, *Plato christianus: Übernahme und Umgestaltung des
Platonismus durch die Väter* (Einsiedeln, 1964), *passim.*

30. In the article "Humanisme," DS, 46–7 (1969), 963–4 and in a more
developed study on "L'humanisme des moines du moyen âge," *Studi
medievali,* 10 (1969), 44–76, I have cited some texts.

B

three foundation stones of this tradition were Plato, Origen, and Evagrius. Through the writings of Cassian, Augustine, Gregory the Great and others, the Platonic, Stoic, and Origenist elements, purified and passed on by Gregory of Nyssa, Evagrius, Maximus, Eriugena and others found their place in new and original syntheses which remained in contact with the earlier sources but which were nonetheless quite different. In some respects they were not so rich, but, on the other hand, were better adapted to the men whom they were to sanctify, and they were enriched with life experience more familiar to them.[31]

In this respect, Evagrius brought about a veritable turnabout—in this sense a "conversion"—of the ideas received from early Hellenism. He did indeed retain what had been given him, but he modified—or more exactly inverted—the values.[32] Where the Stoics began with knowledge—which they called logic or theology—and then went on to the physic, that is to say cosmology, to come at length to *praxis* or ethics, Evagrius began the spiritual itinerary with the latter. His way led man from asceticism to knowledge, and from there to "spiritual doctrine." At the end, at the summit, at the *apex mentis,* there was to be found the knowledge of God "in himself," that is to say in the very deepest depths of the man who had this experience. He did not attain to simply a knowledge of God as it were in a mirror of creation but rather in the real experience of himself being purified and united to him.

Here we have in Evagrius a sort of extreme "Origenism," which is not without its dangers, for according to this viewpoint a man can unite himself directly to the Trinity without the mediation of the Incarnate Word. Certain pages where St Bernard speaks of mystical union make it clear that he knew this point of view,[33] perhaps through Cassian. But the Abbot of Clairvaux was so

---

31. E. von Ivánka, *op. cit.,* 370 and in the Index under the names of the medieval authors.

32. According to E. von Ivánka, *op. cit.,* 146-8.

33. According to E. von Ivánka, *op. cit.,* 148, n. 1, referring to St Bernard, *Sup. Cant.,* 20, 8-9, and to Cassian, *Conf.,* 1:15 and *Conf.,* 12.

impregnated with the whole of the Catholic tradition that he easily avoided the deviation that this could have led to if he isolated from the whole of which it forms a part this idea of the deepest being of man, that which in him is the most intimate and which makes him to be who he is, uniting itself to the source of being. Bernard was able to make use of this heritage from Evagrius, reinterpreting it and situating it in a larger context.

One cannot grasp in all its fullness the teaching of Bernard nor of the other Cistercian authors of that time if one does not know their sources and among them Evagrius.

Evagrius Today

The influence of Evagrius then, whether directly or through intermediaries, remains and continues to grow. Through him the whole of an ancient wisdom, both theoretical and practical, has been transmitted and inserted into life. His texts were at once a terminus and a starting point. They were the culmination of his own experiences, the meeting point of all the trends of his period. At the same time they were also the starting point of a new phase in evolution which has never ceased to go forward. It is easy therefore to understand that such a varied and rich teaching, such a powerful personality as Evagrius, should today merit attention not only from those scholars who edit his texts but also from such deep and original thinkers as Rahner, Hausherr, Balthasar, and Daniélou. And it is just as understandable that simple men of God recognize in his writings a description of their own problems and difficulties and also discover solutions in them. I recall that when I prepared a critical edition of a Latin version of Evagrius' *Sentences for Monks,* based on the Spanish manuscripts, I was asked if the text might be translated into Spanish and published in a small local magazine because the Christians of that region found spiritual nourishment in them. And today I know monks and nuns who draw as much profit from Evagrius as scholars find—according to their historical or psychological standpoint—difficulties or pleasure.

Monastic tradition is not identical with the material transmission of literary documents. Nor does it consist in constantly referring to historical sources. It is rather a living continuity. It is good, therefore, that a monk such as Father Bamberger, who also knows well the theological tradition and is skilled in the work of spiritual direction, can show us how Christian Platonism holds a legitimate place in our thinking today and still has a fruitful role to play. By means of very precise examples he illustrates that humanism which is the heritage of an earlier monasticism, a monasticism which was open to all the values of philosophical thinking. To all that he had received from philosophy Evagrius joined the psychological experience of generations of monks, and it is this alliance of reflection with life that makes his writings so valuable today.

Men must live in their own day, be of their own times, in such-wise that perennial problems may receive the benefit of scientific advance in all domains, but especially in that of psychology. It is difficult to anticipate what new elements will be brought forth as these texts are examined under new lights. But it is already obvious that when a psychiatrist studies them he finds in them things which escape the simple historian. Father Bamberger established this in his article in which philology was made to serve very up-to-date views on human experience.[34] A similar study has also come from the pen of Father Canivet, sj.[35] From a sixth-century text, "The Life of St Theodosus," he was able to bring out traces of "erroneous asceticism," diagnose disturbances of the mind, and admire therapy which led those who considered themselves abandoned by God to patience and thanksgiving. In his introduction to the text presented in this volume, Father Bamberger alludes to similarities which have been pointed out between Evagrius on the one hand and St John of the Cross and Freud on the other. What we need today is not only critical editions and philo-

---

34. J. E. Bamberger, "*ΜΝΗΜΕ-ΔΙΑΘΕΣΙΣ*: The Psychic Dynamism in the Ascetical Theology of St Basil," OCP 34 (1968), 233–51.

35. *Recherches des sciences religieuses*, 50 (1962), 161–205.

logical exegesis of the ancient sources but present-day and constantly reviewed studies of the states of soul which are part of the spiritual experience of every age. The ancient writers have some very real contribution to make to our understanding of the facts of our own personal existence. It is not a matter, of course, of projecting our own ideas into the documents of the past in order to make them say what they did not intend to say. Rather, it is a question of beginning with these ancient witnesses and seeing if they have something to teach us about ourselves, about what we are today. In this respect one can anticipate very fruitful results from the younger generation of research workers who are better prepared for what we call inter-disciplinary work. There are already promising signs of this, and Father Bamberger gives us a further one in this volume.

Father Bamberger was a disciple of a master of the monastic life and spiritual teaching who was one of the geniuses of our times: Thomas Merton. It is he who should have written this preface, for it was he who first encouraged this translation. In many of his own essays he showed an excelling ability to rejuvenate ancient texts and bring to light all the freshness of early documents. Into apparently dry bones he breathed new life, the intense life which was his own. His existence was a constant discovery of life. In one of the last books which he prepared for publication he compared the sayings of ancient Christian monks and the words, proverbs, and riddles of monks of Zen Buddhism, both ancient and new.[36] In the present-day climate, when the monks of different religions are beginning to enter into dialogue with one another, to discover each other, a publication such as we have here is most opportune. It will reveal to many that wisdom which God created for all ages and confided to mortal man. In the course of its being handed on from father to son, from generation to generation, it does at times become obscure and covered over with the dust of human thought.

36. *Zen and the Birds of Appetite* (New York, 1968), 99–100. On p. 131 we read: "This is the language of Evagrius Ponticus, severely intellectual, a fact which brings him closer to Zen than the more affective theologians of prayer. . . ."

But such accidents of time and deeds can never prevent this God-given wisdom from leading to God those who truly seek him, for "in every generation wisdom lives in holy souls and makes them friends of God."[37]

J. Leclercq OSB

Clervaux Abbey, Luxembourg

37. Wis 7:27.

INTRODUCTION

THE TWO WORKS OF EVAGRIUS PONTICUS which are translated in this volume have played a notable role in the spiritual life of the Church as well as in the development of mystical and ascetical theology. Their influence has been active, above all in the monastic world, from the fourth century, when they were composed, down to the present day.

RECOVERY OF THE EVAGRIAN WRITINGS

Until recent times Evagrius was hardly more than an obscure name in the annals of history. His very memory was all but forgotten except insofar as it was linked with that of Origen, in a series of condemnations of their more extreme theological views.[1] In spite of several learned works written on him at the end of the

---

1. Origen (185–253) was the most influential and brilliant writer of the early Church. He lived and taught first in Alexandria then in Palestine. His vast literary output covered the fields of textual criticism, homilies, scriptural commentaries and important theological works. Although his theological ideas early became controversial and finally condemned by the Fifth Ecumenical Council, by reason of his excellence and rare piety he continued to exert a profound influence upon the later Patristic Age and the Middle Ages. His ascetic teaching provided the theoretic basis for monastic theology in large part. Not only Evagrius but also the three Cappadocian Fathers were marked by Origen's teaching. For an evaluation of his life and works and a bibliography see J. Quasten, *Patrology*, vol. 2 (Westminster, Md., 1955), 37–101.

last century,[2] the prevailing view fifty years ago was that Evagrius was an able teacher who left us some interesting, if not very impressive, literary works.[3]

At present, however, there is a completely different attitude toward Evagrius and his works. He is now looked upon as the author who has produced "one of the most captivating works of Christian antiquity"[4] and as "one of the most important names in the history of spirituality, one of those that not only marked a decisive turning-point, but called forth a real spiritual mutation."[5]

The recovery of his lost writings and of his life-story is hailed as "a romance of modern scholarship,"[6] and not without good reason. There is, however, a certain irony in it as well, for it reveals how his name was reviled as that of a heretic[7] even while his teaching was being preached and spread abroad in the most serious religious circles. At times it was his very detractors who were the most influenced by his writings.

Before studying his life and works in detail let us take a brief look into the causes and events which led to his condemnation and the prolonged eclipse of his name.

2. Notably that by O. Zöckler, *Evagrius Pontikus, Seine Stellung in der altchristlichen Literatur-und Dogmengeschichte* (Munich, 1893); also the article by J. Dräseke, "Zu Evagrios Pontikos," *Zeitshcrift für wissenschaftliche Theologie,* 37 (1894), 125–37.

3. The article in the voluminous DTC by P. Godet is very brief (2 columns) and makes no attempt to describe the particulars of his teaching, his theological antecedents or his place in the spiritual theology of the Church. The reason is that at that time the available works were too fragmentary and limited to allow for this kind of assessment. See DTC, 5:1611f.

4. J. Daniélou, in a review of A. Guillaumont's edition of the *Kephalaia Gnostica* published in 1958; see RSR, 47 (1959), 115.

5. L. Bouyer, *The Spirituality of the New Testament and the Fathers,* vol. 1 (New York, 1963), 381.

6. O. Chadwick, *John Cassian: A study in primitive monasticism* (Cambridge, 1950), 82. The second edition of this work (Cambridge, 1968) ascribes to Evagrius the title of "father of our literature of spirituality," p. 86.

7. In particular St Maximus the Confessor, who owes so much to Evagrian thought, has nothing good to say about him, and "heretic" is the only distinctive title he reserves for him. See M. Viller, "Aux Sources de la Spiritualité de S. Maxime," RAM, 11 (1930), 159.

Ecclesiastical Condemnation

Evagrius was an ardent Origenist. He speculated at great length upon certain of the more daring of Origen's teachings, such as the doctrine of pre-existence of souls and the doctrine of the eventual return of all souls, even those of the demons, to the primitive union with Divinity (ἀποκατάστασις). It is not so certain that Origen himself held some of these points at the end of his life. In any case, he was quite careful to express his submission to the Church's judgment on their orthodoxy. Evagrius was less cautious. As Von Balthasar has pointed out, Evagrius tended to pursue principles to their extreme logical conclusions and then proceeded to adopt them in this extreme form as norms for life.[8]

The inevitable happened. Evagrius joined Origen and Didymus the Blind[9] on the list of heretics. The first official condemnation was at the Fifth Ecumenical Council in 553, while Justinian the Great was ruling the Byzantine Empire. The next three Ecumenical Councils that met made it a part of their business to repeat this same condemnation.[10]

It is now known that the chief target of the anathemas of the

8. H. U. von Balthasar, "Metaphysik und Mystik des Evagrius Ponticus," *Zeitschrift für Askeze und Mystik,* 14 (1939), 32.

9. Didymus the Blind (313–about 398) was a man of remarkable gifts and intellectual accomplishments in spite of the blindness which he suffered from his youth. Under the great Athanasius he headed the Catechetical School that had formerly been the theater of Origen's activity. Both St Jerome and Rufinus were numbered among his pupils. There can be little doubt that Evagrius knew him personally and accompanied by his disciples visited him in his cell on the outskirts of Alexandria. See Palladius, *The Lausiac History,* trans. R. Meyer, ACW, 34 (1964), 35. (Hereafter cited as LH.) For bibliography and further details on his writings, see Quasten, *op. cit.,* vol. 3, 85–100.

10. For this history see DTC, 11:1565ff.: "Origenisme." The dates of these Councils are as follows: Sixth—680 AD; Seventh—781 AD; Eighth—869 AD. In addition, at the Lateran Synod of 649 AD, which was attended by St Maximus the Confessor, Evagrius was once again condemned. At the important Synod *in trullo,* held in 692 AD to complete the works undertaken by the Fifth and Sixth Councils, this condemnation was ratified. See further A. Guillaumont, *Les "Kephalaia Gnostica" d'Evagre le Pontique* (Paris, 1962), 136f. (Hereafter cited as Guillaumont.)

Councils were certain Christological doctrines found in a particular work of Evagrius known as the *Kephalaia Gnostica*.[11] These same doctrines are not found in many of his other works, especially in his more pastoral writings. Perhaps the only other major work of his which is strongly marked by these theories in their extreme form is his *Commentary on the Psalms*.[12]

As a result of this official condemnation the *Kephalaia Gnostica* were, on orders of Justinian,[13] destroyed in their original Greek version. They were preserved, however, sufficiently long for some Syriac translations to be made. This work is extant only in the Syriac translation, and the Armenian which is made from the Syriac.[14] Thus was preserved for us the most important of all of Evagrius' theoretic writings. There are two distinct translations of the Syriac. The "received version," the only one known till recently, is actually a very able modification of the text. It is purged of much of its objectionable Christology. The version recently discovered is much more faithful to the original text, and for that reason allows us for the first time in more than a thousand years to study the Evagrian systematic theology in its original lineaments.[15]

11. For Evagrius' Christology see Guillaumont, 156–9; also F. Refoulé, "La christologie d'Evagre et l'Origenisme," *OCP*, 27 (1961), 221–66.

12. See Refoulé, *ibid.,* 241f.

13. The whole affair was initiated and energetically guided through the Council by the Emperor. In fact, the Council's part was largely to ratify, by acclamation, the letter of Justinian which contained the anathemas. See Guillaumont, 135f.

14. See Guillaumont, 256. The Syriac translations were done very early. The one made by Philoxenus of Mabboug antedates the condemnation of the Council by about fifty years, having been made around the year 500. Some of the Evagrian writings were translated several times into Syriac and the various versions are still extant, as Muyldermans has stressed in his analysis of the Syriac manuscript tradition. See his *Evagriana Syriaca* (Louvain, 1952), 46f and *passim*. (Hereafter cited as ES.) That the Armenian translation is largely dependent upon the Syriac (only some parts of the Greek text were available to the translators) is demonstrated by Hausherr, "Les Versions Syriaque et Arménienne d'Evagre le Pontique," *Orientalia Christiana,* 22 (1931), 114.

15. Guillaumont, 256f.

Some other writings of Evagrius managed to survive in Greek by passing as the work of a more evidently orthodox Father. His *Commentary on the Psalms* was transmitted under the name of Origen and thus, in spite of the Christological heresies it contains,[16] was preserved in Greek.

His more pastoral works fared better at the hands of posterity than his dogmatic writings. They have been more largely transmitted in the original Greek version for they were early accepted by wide segments of the Church and eagerly read without anyone finding objectionable theories in them.[17] It is to this group of pastoral works that the two collections of sentences translated in this volume belong. Both were much admired and widely influential in the period immediately following Evagrius' death.

In this way it happened that, even while his name was execrated as that of an abominable heretic by some, Evagrius was loved and esteemed as a sure and holy spiritual guide by large segments of the Church. This ambiguity was to adhere to his memory throughout the centuries.

In the West Evagrius enjoyed a wide popularity at first. St Jerome observes[18] that Evagrius was being read by large numbers of Christians in the Latin translation made by Rufinus.[19] These

16. See von Balthasar, "Die Hiera des Evagrius Pontikus," *Zeitschrift für katholische Theologie*, 63 (1939), 86–106 and 181–206; also M. J. Rondeau, "Le Commentaire sur les Psaumes d'Evagre le Pontique," *OCP*, 26 (1960), 307–48.

17. In this context the story told about the much-consulted Barsanupheus, the great spiritual director who lived in Palestine in the neighborhood of Gaza (died about 540 AD), is very informative. When asked about the advisability of reading Evagrius by a young monk the elder told him that only his dogmatic works are to be avoided; his other writings if read with discretion can prove very useful for the spiritual life. It is not without significance that this same young monk on another occasion asked the master how it came about that some of the more fervent monks occupied themselves with the works of Evagrius indiscriminately, whether dogmatic or not. Cf. PG 86:898A.

18. The *Epistle to Ctesiphon*, 133:3, PL 22:1151A.

19. Rufinus of Aquileia was a close friend of St Jerome from their student days in Rome. After the completion of his studies he spent some years in a monastery at Aquileia as a monk, once again in the company of Jerome. When Melania went to Egypt on her way to the Holy Land in 371 Rufinus

works were published a year or two after Evagrius' death in 399,[20] but before the fifth century was ended a second translation of certain writings was made by the historian Gennadius.[21]

Because the years between Evagrius' death and his condemnation in 553 were precisely the decisive years for determining the character and spirit of Western monasticism, and because his writings were so popularly received in the West at this time, he has proved to be one of the significant influences upon the Latin monastic tradition.[22] Even after his condemnation, when there was a sharp decrease in the circulation of his writings,[23] he continued to have an active though indirect influence through the writings of his disciple, John Cassian.[24] But his direct influence was eliminated almost completely for more than a millennium once he was labeled

---

accompanied her and assisted her in the founding of the double monastery in Jerusalem, on the Mount of Olives. Both became ardent students of Origen, and Rufinus dedicated his talents as a translator to a number of Origen's more important works, and thereby preserved them for posterity. The friendship that grew up between him and Evagrius when the latter was a guest at the Jerusalem hospice attached to Melania's monastery was maintained by letters and presumably by their mutual interest in Origenist theology. Some of these letters have survived (see Guillaumont, 69f.). In particular Rufinus translated into Latin Evagrius' *Sentences for Monks* and *Praktikos*. The works of Rufinus are printed in PL 21. For other details of his life and a bibliography, see B. Altaner, *Patrology,* trans. H. Graef (New York, 1960), 459ff.

20. O. Bardenhewer, *Geschichte der altkirchlichen Literatur,* vol. 3 (Freiburg, 1923), 555.

21. See *De viribus illustris,* 11, PL 58:1067A. Gennadius also translated the *Antirrheticus* of Evagrius, although this translation is now lost.

22. See the informative discussion by A. Wilmart, "Les versions latines des Sentences d'Evagre pour les Vierges," *Revue Bénédictine,* 28 (1911), 152. The earlier Latin version of these Sentences, published by Jean Leclercq in *Scriptorium,* 5 (1951), 195–213, has allowed this same investigator to trace the spread of Evagrian influence in the Latin West in considerable detail. See his *The Love of Learning and the Desire for God* (New York, 1961), 117. On the nature of this influence, which was practical rather than theoretical, see his judicious remarks on p. 116.

23. Wilmart, *ibid.*

24. For the marked influence of Evagrius upon Cassian see the basic work of S. Marsili, *Giovanni Cassiano ed Evagrio Pontico* (Rome, 1936). Basically Cassian derives his teaching on a number of the central ideas in his works from Evagrius although he does not mention his name, for reasons of prudence.

as an Origenist by the Church. In this the Latin world was more absolute and efficient than was the Greek.

But even in the West his name was preserved, at least in those monasteries where the exploits and teachings of the early Egyptian monks were read in one of the numerous Latin versions of the *Lausiac History* of Palladius,[25] or in that other famous account of the desert fathers preserved in the *Historia Monachorum*,[26] another work translated by Rufinus. But this meant hardly more than that Evagrius was remembered as a rather dim figure from the glorious past, a holy man, a gifted teacher but one whose works had been lost to posterity.[27]

---

25. Palladius (c. 363–431) is the chief source of our information on Evagrius. He was born in Galatia and at the age of twenty-three became a monk in the monastery founded by Rufinus on the Mount of Olives. He moved from there to Jericho for a time and then on to Alexandria. Finally he settled in Nitria where he became a disciple of Evagrius whom he followed to Cells. After the death of Evagrius he was forced to leave Egypt because of his health and thus it came about that he went to Constantinople where he became fast friends with John Chrysostom. He was ordained Bishop of Helenopolis and remained a loyal friend to Chrysostom, not fearing to pay for his loyalty with much suffering. He wrote two works which enjoyed lasting renown: *The Dialogue* which deals with Chrysostom and the *Lausiac History* which gives an account of the lives of many of the more heroic figures of the Egyptian desert. It seems quite likely that Palladius had written a biography of Evagrius of greater length and that the details preserved in chapter thirty-eight of his *Lausiac History* is a brief résumé of this work. The Syriac version of this history may well contain original material derived from this now lost longer biographical account of Evagrius. For further discussion see Guillaumont, 76, n. 118. It is now well established that the *Lausiac History* is fundamentally conceived in the spirit of the Evagrian theological system. Cf. R. Draguet, "L'Histoire Lausiaque, une oeuvre ecrite dans l'esprit d'Evagre," *Revue d'histoire ecclésiastique*, 41 (1946), 321–64 and 42 (1947), 5–49.

26. The *Historia Monachorum* is likewise an early monastic history composed chiefly of biographical accounts of the more notable figures of the Egyptian desert. It was composed around the year 400 perhaps by Timothy, the Archdeacon of Alexandria, a contemporary of Evagrius. Rufinus translated it from Greek into Latin and, since it gives a favorable account of Evagrius, in this way too Rufinus contributed to spreading Evagrian influence in the Latin Church. For bibliography see Quasten, vol. 3, 178. A new critical edition has recently come out: A. J. Festugière, *Historia Monachorum in Aegypto* (Subsidia Hagiographica 34, Brussels, 1961).

27. Wilmart, *op. cit.,* 146, has pointed out how few Mss. of the Latin

Aside from the publication in the late seventeenth century of his *Sentences for Monks* and the *Exhortation to a Virgin* by Holstenius[28] and of the *Praktikos* together with a few other collections of sentences by Cotelier[29] a few years later, nothing of importance was done to recover the place of Evagrius in the history of spirituality until the publication of *Evagrius Pontikus* by Zöckler in the late nineteenth century. The early years of the twentieth century saw the publication of a number of newly discovered works of Evagrius. The first was the Armenian corpus of Evagrius, which included a biographical note on Evagrius as well as an extensive collection of his more important works. This was published in 1907 by Sarghisian,[30] but because the whole work was in Armenian it had rather little influence at first. The publication by Frankenberg, however, of the Syriac translation of many of Evagrius' basic writings together with a retroversion into Greek some five years later[31] led to a considerable quickening of interest in our author. When Gressman published the original Greek text of the *Sentences to Monks* and the *Exhortation to a Virgin* the next year[32] enough material was available for a rather extensive and thorough study of the main lines of Evagrius' system. It was Bousset who supplied

---

translation of the once popular *Exhortation to a Virgin* now remain. As late as 1908 one of the best informed scholars of the period wrote of the Evagrian corpus: "Only a few brief and broken fragments have reached us." See O. Bardenhewer, *Patrology,* trans. T. Sheehan (St Louis, 1908, 2nd ed.), 310.

28. Lucas Holstenius, *Codex Regularum,* 6 vols. (Gräz reprint of the 1759 ed. of Augsburg, 1957). The works of Evagrius are printed in vol. 1, 465–69.

29. The *Praktikos* was discovered and edited, poorly it is true, by J. B. Cotelier in 1686. It is this edition which is reprinted in Migne.

30. H. B. Sarghisian, *The Life and Works of the Holy Father Evagrius Pontikus in an Armenian Version of the Fifth Century with Introduction and Notes* (Venice, 1907).

31. W. Frankenberg, "Evagrius Pontikus," *Abhandlungen der königlichen Gesellschaft der Wissenschaften zu Göttingen, Phil.-hist.* Klasse, N.F. XIII, 2 (Berlin, 1912).

32. H. Gressmann, *Nonnenspiegel und Mönchsspiegel des Euagrios Pontikos zum ersten Male in der Urschrift herausgegeben* (Texte und Untersuchungen 39, 4B, Leipzig, 1913).

this basic study in 1923.[33] At the same time he discovered that the important dogmatic letter of St Basil, the eighth letter as it is known, was actually authored by Evagrius. His results were independently confirmed by R. Melcher's publication, at the same time, of his book which vindicates this eighth letter of St Basil for Evagrius.[34]

But the real break-through came in 1930 when M. Viller demonstrated the very basic influence exercised by Evagrius upon one of the most important of Byzantine theologians, St Maximus the Confessor.[35] No one apparently had previously suspected this influence since St Maximus not only did nothing to indicate his dependence upon Evagrius but actually had spoken of him as an "abominable heretic."[36] Later studies have shown that Viller was over-impressed with the extent of influence that Evagrius had upon St Maximus.[37] But the basic fact of a considerable influence has

33. W. Bousset, *Apophthegmata* (Tübingen, 1922), III. Buch: "Euagrios-studien."

34. Melcher, *Der achte Brief des heiligen Basilius ein Werk des Evagrius Pontikus* (Münster, 1923).

35. Viller, *art. cit.,* 156–84, 239–68. The significance of this article was appreciated immediately by such investigators as I. Hausherr and the young Karl Rahner. The latter wrote an article on Evagrius which he modestly described as little more than a paraphrase in German of Viller's article, "Die geistliche Lehre des Evagrius Pontikus," *ZAM*, 8 (1933), 21–38.

36. Viller, *ibid.,* 159, where Maximus is quoted as using the word "impious" or "faithless." Of course, at this time Evagrius was thought of as a man anathematized by the Church since Maximus wrote after the condemnation of 553. Maximus (580–662) was a member of the nobility of Constantinople and while still young had become a member of the court, serving as secretary to the Emperor. Before long, however, he left all to become a monk in a nearby monastery, and attained to renown by virtue of his writings. He was the leading theologian of his age, and fought strenuously for the true faith against the powerful faction that favored the monothelite Christology. Finally he triumphed in the struggle when in 649 the Lateran Synod condemned mono-thelitism. This same Synod condemned Evagrius once again, so it is not too surprising that Maximus tended to speak of Evagrius in harsh terms. Towards the end of his life Maximus was subjected to cruel tortures for his defense of Orthodoxy and soon after this ordeal died as a result of his treatment. For further details and bibliographical data see Altaner, *op. cit.,* 629–33.

37. P. Sherwood, *St Maximus the Confessor*, ACW, 21 (1955), 235, n. 356; also W. Völker, 490ff. *Maximus Confessor als Meister des geistlichen Lebens*

been well established and proved to be the decisive discovery needed to assure for Evagrius recognition of his importance as a spiritual writer. Since Viller's publication there have been increasing numbers of articles dealing with the many questions involved in establishing the place of Evagrius in the life of the Church.

A few of the major contributions deserve to be mentioned here briefly so as to complete the history of the recovery of the writings of Evagrius. A few years after Viller's paper Hausherr published a careful study of the *Chapters on Prayer,* which until that time had been ascribed to St Nilus of Sinai.[38] His conclusions were that the true author of the work was Evagrius Ponticus not St Nilus, and that the work contained some of the most important theological concepts on prayer in the history of spirituality.[39] In particular he demonstrated that Evagrius was the writer responsible for the popularization of the works of Origen and Gregory of Nyssa, but still more significantly he had devised and shaped a highly personal synthesis of spirituality into a fully articulated and systematized view of the whole spiritual life. Hausherr further drew the conclusion that Evagrius is the chief source of the properly contemplative spirituality of the Byzantine tradition, to such an extent that its centuries old tradition should properly be described as Evagrian spirituality[40] not, as he had formerly recommended, Sinaitic spirituality.[41]

The next major contribution came from Hans Urs von Balthasar

(Wiesbaden, 1965). This author makes the point that Maximus formed his own theology even while he took elements from Evagrius and other earlier writers.

38. St Nilus of Sinai (died about 430), the *higoumenos* of a monastery in Ancyra (modern Ankara, the capital of present-day Turkey), was a famous and influential spiritual writer who was much influenced by St John Chrysostom. There is still confusion as to the extent of his writings, and some of the works ascribed to him by certain Mss. may well belong to Evagrius. The *Chapters on Prayer* long passed as the work of St Nilus.

39. *RAM,* 15 (1934), 169–70.

40. I. Hausherr, "Oraison Hesychaste," *Orientalia Christiana,* 9 (1927), 134ff.

41. I. Hausherr, *RAM,* 15 (1934), 169.

in 1939.[42] He made a detailed study of the *Commentary on the Psalms* ascribed to Origen and arrived at the conclusion that this work was actually in large part the work of Evagrius. He based his judgment exclusively on internal evidence. In 1960 the correctness of his view was demonstrated when Rondeau discovered a Vatican manuscript which provided evidence that the work indeed came from the hand of Evagrius.[43]

The crowning achievement came in 1952 when A. and C. Guillaumont reported the discovery of the original, unexpurgated version of Evagrius' *magnum opus*, the *Kephalaia Gnostica*.[44] This work was preserved in a Syriac translation, and was found to contain precisely those Christological doctrines which were condemned by the Fifth Ecumenical Council as being Origenist.[45] Since the publication in 1958[46] of this authentic version it has been possible to re-evaluate Evagrius on a much broader scale precisely as a dogmatic theologian. He has emerged from this study as the author of one of the works "most characteristic of Christian Neoplatonism," who leads us to "the supreme limits of the adventure of the spirit which advances in absolute solitude in search of intelligible light. But this light for Evagrius is that of the Trinity."[47]

---

42. H. U. von Balthasar, "Die Hiera des Evagrius Pontikus," *Zeitschrift für katholische Theologie*, 63 (1939), 86–106 and 181–206. At the same time he published a second article studying very thoroughly the Evagrian thought: "Metaphysik und Mystik des Evagrius Pontikus," *ZAM*, 14 (1939), 31–47. This last article has been recently translated into English by a monk of Gethsemane Abbey, *Monastic Studies*, 3 (1965), 183–95.

43. M. J. Rondeau, "Le Commentaire sur les Psaumes d'Evagre le Pontique," *OCP*, 26 (1960), 307–48. An edition of this commentary is being prepared by the same author on the basis of the newly discovered manuscript *Vat Graec* 754 (tenth century). F. Refoulé has studied the Christology of this work which he states should be considered rather a series of marginal notes, or *scolia*, than a true commentary. "La christologie d'Evagre et l'Origenisme," *OCP*, 27 (1961), 241.

44. A. and C. Guillaumont, "Le texte véritable des 'Gnostica' d'Evagre le Pontique," *Revue d'histoire des religions*, 142 (1952), 156–205.

45. F. Refoulé, *op. cit.*, 251–55.

46. A. Guillaumont, *Les "Kephalaia Gnostica" d'Evagre le Pontique* (Paris, 1958).

47. J. Daniélou, *RSR*, 47 (1959), 115, in a review of the work cited in the preceding note.

C

As we shall soon discover, the final word has not as yet been spoken on the definitive position occupied by Evagrius in tradition. While there is wide agreement at present on his filling a pivotal role in the transmission and development of the ascetic and mystical theology of both the East and the West, the precise degree of influence is far from being clearly established. Perhaps the most important problem to be solved at the present is the nature of the relationship between the more speculative and Hellenistic side of his thought on the one hand and the more practical aspect which derives from his own experience and from his having entered so deeply into the Coptic desert tradition. In spite of the thoroughness and penetration of Guillaumont's study of the *Kephalaia Gnostica*[48] he seems to have given too little attention to the more traditional elements of the Evagrian corpus. No one so far has been able to reconcile in any kind of convincing synthesis these two blocks of material to be found in the various works of the monk-theologian. Indeed, one finds opposite conclusions drawn about his qualities by different scholars depending upon which work of his they concentrate upon. Wilmart speaks of him as a great director who had a strong sense for the practical demands of the spiritual life;[49] Von Balthasar has pointed out that his greatest defects are his tendency to be too rigid in adhering to system and to form extreme positions.[50]

At the present nothing is clearer than that the key to understanding the widely disparate components of Evagrius' teaching and personality remains hidden from us. One has the impression that the two major streams of influence, the Hellenistic and the Coptic, flow side by side, in mutual isolation, rather than merging into a single confluence. Yet it is abundantly evident that to his disciples Evagrius represented the very pattern of restored integrity in all senses of that word. He was considered to have attained to a rare

48. Guillaumont's work is easily the most complete study of Evagrius so far undertaken. He himself is aware, however, that he has not yet given a full picture of Evagrius and his thought; Guillaumont, 337, especially note 8.

49. A. Wilmart, *op. cit.*, 152.

50. H. U. von Balthasar, "Metaphysik und Mystik des Evagrius Ponticus," *ZAM*, 14 (1939), 32.

degree of harmony in his personality through his ascetic practice and through his pure prayer.[51]

There remains then an aura of mystery surrounding the figure of Evagrius. Any attempt to portray him now can only claim to be a preliminary sketch. The definitive portrait must await another day.

LIFE

Evagrius was born in 345 in the small provincial town of Ibora in Pontus.[52] His father was a chorbishop,[53] that is to say, a bishop of a country area who traveled about to care for the various churches

51. LH 38:13, p. 114.

52. Ibora, present-day Iverönü in Turkey (see R. Janin, *Dictionnaire d'Histoire et de Geographie Ecclésiastique*, 16 (1964), 107: "Evagre le Pontique") was placed under the episcopal jurisdiction of Gregory of Nyssa in 380 AD. Gregory visited here to preside over the election of a new bishop, and it seems very likely that the retiring bishop was Evagrius senior, the father of Evagrius Ponticus. We know from Palladius that Evagrius' father died while the son was in the Egyptian desert and, to judge from the degree of spiritual discernment the story told by Palladius implies, he must have been there for some time. (See *LH*, 38:13, p. 114; also the *Praktikos*, 95.) For the visit of Gregory to Ibora see his *Epistle 19*, PG 46:1076C. The name of Evagrius senior is known from an epistle of Gregory Nazianzen while he was tutor to Evagrius. He wrote the letter to the father and in the course of it mentions that it was for the sake of Evagrius' religious education that he, Gregory, had charge of his son (see *Epistle 3*, PG 37:24B; see also Sozomen, *Historia Ecclesiastica*, VI, 30 and Guillaumont, 49, note 8, who has pointed out the significance of Gregory's letter).

Sozomen provides an interesting variant in the account of Evagrius' origins which is not without significance for the history of spirituality. He maintains that Evagrius was a native of Iberia (modern Georgia, USSR), not Ibora. (See PG 67:1384.) The earliest Coptic version of the *Lausiac History* affirms the same origin for Evagrius. The Georgians consider Evagrius to be their first monk and honor him accordingly. Cf. M. Tarchnisvili, "Il monachesimo Georgiano nelle sue Orienti e nei suoi Primi Sviluppi," *Il Monachesimo Orientale*, Orientalia Christiana Analecta, 153 (Rome, 1958), 307.

53. LH 38:2, p. 110. A χωρεπίσκοπος is a bishop with all the essential powers of the episcopal order but whose faculty of exercising these powers is limited. In the early Church he would confer minor orders only. His functions were supervised by his metropolitan. Although the office was quite common in the patristic age, today it is almost solely an honorary title. See LH, p. 200, note 340.

committed to his care but whose powers were somewhat restricted. Ibora was only a short distance from the family estate of St Basil which was located at Annesi. There Basil had retired for a time to live the ascetic life. It is hardly surprising then to learn that Evagrius fell under the influence of St Basil while he was still quite young. It was Basil who ordained him lector.[54] It may have been at this moment that Evagrius considered taking the monastic habit. Monasticism was perhaps the most vital movement in Pontus at that period for it had both Basil and his friend Gregory Nazianzen as inspiring and dynamic leaders. But it seems that the young Evagrius decided against joining the movement[55] possibly because

54. LH 38:2, p. III. St Basil (c. 330–379), called the Great already in his lifetime, was the recognized leader of the Church in Asia Minor during the period between 350 AD and his death, the years of Evagrius' youth. It was Basil's basic policy which prevailed at the Second Ecumenical Council, partly through the implementation given to it by Gregory of Nazianzen and Evagrius himself. Basil played the predominant role also in the monastic revival that took place in his province at this time, and in some sense has been considered the Father of the monks of the Byzantine world. Through the great influence he had upon his intimate friend Gregory Nazianzen and his younger brother Gregory of Nyssa, both of whom he inspired to enter upon a serious spiritual life in the spirit of the "new monasticism," he was to extend his personal influence still further. These three friends, known as the Cappadocian Fathers, represent one of the high-points of Christianity by reason of their holiness, character and culture. All three are numbered among the greatest theologians of the Church. Evagrius is indebted to each of them to different degrees for much of his doctrine. For further details see Quasten, *op. cit.,* vol. 3, 204–36 for Basil; pp. 236–54 for Gregory Nazianzen and pp. 254–96 for Gregory of Nyssa.

55. W. Bousset had concluded that it was from Basil that Evagrius had taken the monastic habit and had fled from the community of his profession from a sense of oppression deriving from the emphasis on practical, social activity so characteristic of Basil's monastic establishment. But this argument, based as it was on the assumption that Evagrius' Letter twenty-two was written to Basil, makes for little conviction once it is accepted that it in fact is addressed in all probability to Melania and the brethren on the Mount of Olives. See Guillaumont, 69–70, note 92. According to the Greek text of LH there is serious reason to think that Evagrius received the habit from Melania (see ACW 34, 113; but for a different interpretation see the note on this passage in the same work, note 347, p. 201) at least a second time. There are reasons, though, for thinking the first conferral of the habit came from Basil.

he felt somewhat repelled by the practical emphasis given to the monastic system erected by Basil. He was more attracted by the stimulating intellectual life of the capital, Constantinople, than by the socially oriented activities of the Basilian foundations.[56]

The next thing we know for certain about Evagrius is that he was ordained deacon by Gregory Nazianzen, shortly after the death of Basil, in 379.[57] Not too long afterwards Gregory, who was the bishop of Sasima, a small town in Pontus, was called upon to restore the Nicene faith in the capital city, hitherto for some years a stronghold of Arianism. He invited Evagrius to join him, in the capacity of archdeacon. When the Second Ecumenical Council was assembled there in 381 Gregory especially made use of the services of the brilliant young deacon whose powers were placing him in the forefront of the struggle for the Nicene faith. It was his many gifts which commended Evagrius to Gregory. Perceiving "his perspicacity and his great skill in the Divine Books and recognizing that he was a very virtuous man in control of all his passions he (Gregory) elevated him to the deaconate."[58] A genuine affection grew up between the two men which would last throughout the lives of both. In his last years Evagrius still spoke with deep respect for his former mentor.[59] That Gregory shared these same

---

56. The operation of orphanages and of hospitals was considered by Basil to be ideal monastic work. He also gives much importance to obedience and both of these features, in the form they assume under his hand, distinguish his type of monasticism from that of the desert fathers. See Bouyer, *op. cit.*, 335ff. for a sensitive study of Basil's monastic teaching; also see the *Long Rules* of St Basil in *St Basil: The Ascetical Works*, trans. M. Wagner (Washington, 1953), 223ff. However, it has recently been pointed out that Basil by no means neglected the contemplative aspect of the monastic life, although some scholars, Bousset among them, assert the contrary. See B. Drask, "Beschauliches und tätiges Leben in Mönchtum nach der Lehre Basilius des Grossen," *Freiburger Zeitschrift für Phil. und Theol.*, 7 (1960), 297–309 and 391–414; 8 (1961), 93–108, as reviewed in *The Message of Monastic Spirituality*, A. Louf *et al.*, trans. Monks of New Melleray (Dubuque, 1963), 38.

57. LH 38:2, p. 111.

58. E. A. W. Budge, *The Book of Paradise* (London, 1904), vol. 1, 340.

59. *Praktikos*, 100.

sentiments is evident from his *Testament* in which he gives expression to the gratitude he felt for the loyal friendship of Evagrius.[60]

The Council met in 381, the same year that the Emperor, Theodosius, made his triumphal entrance into the capital. One of the first acts of the Council was to make Gregory its president. In spite of the very serious difficulties and the eventual failure of Gregory to control the various parties represented at the Council, Evagrius was a striking success. When Gregory chose to retire once again to the monastic life he left his assistant, Evagrius, behind, for the new bishop of Constantinople, Nectarius, wished to employ him as archdeacon. "When the blessed Nectarius, Bishop of Constantinople, met him (Evagrius) he was drawn to love him because he saw that he was a man of strong character. So he attached him to himself. In fact Evagrius was loved by everyone and held in honor by all."[61]

Nectarius' protégé did not fail to live up to his expectations. By his preaching and vigorous action he doubtless did much to assure the eventual victory of the policies of St Basil and of Gregory Nazianzen. He soon was known as the "destroyer of the twaddle of the heretics."[62]

At the same time the young preacher found the opportunity to make many friends in the capital. Gregory of Nyssa, the brother of St Basil and himself a bishop, gave the opening address at the Council.[63] No doubt he and Evagrius spent a great deal of time discussing the theology and political questions agitating the Church at that moment in her history.[64] Gregory had made a deep impres-

---

60. PG 37:393B. As Guillaumont has emphasized, this document bears eloquent witness to the intimate friendship existing between Evagrius and Gregory. Nothing could commend Evagrius' basic qualities of mind and spirit more than this relation with Gregory.

61. Budge, *ibid*.

62. A. J. Festugière, *Historia Monachorum in Aegypto* (Brussels, 1961), 123.

63. See the *Sermon on his Ordination* (PG 46:544–553) which J. Daniélou has pointed out and discussed in his work *From Glory to Glory*, trans. H. Musurillo (New York, 1961), 6, note 19.

64. After the death of Basil his brother Gregory of Nyssa felt strongly that he was expected to carry through Basil's policies. It was doubtless all the more

sion at the Court and the Basileus chose him to be Imperial Coun-
cillor.[65] Doubtless he and Evagrius also discussed some of the problems
of the spiritual life which Gregory had treated of in his writings. It
seems very likely that it was at this period that the theological
views which Evagrius would take from Gregory of Nyssa came to
his knowledge and were first reflected upon. If he had read of them
before, his close association with the renowned author-bishop
would have impressed them more deeply upon his mind.[66]

As Evagrius continued in his ministry and his success grew, he
seems to have found considerable satisfaction in the social prominence and the intellectual excitement of the metropolis. What
penchant he had by nature for meditation, quiet and prayer waned.
He grew careless, worldly and delicate. He was "great in pomp,
made a great deal of caring for his body and had himself ministered
to by slaves."[67] Yet he did not altogether neglect his duties as a
cleric. He merely compromised with them, taking advantage of the
"legitimate satisfactions" offered by worldly success. He was
careful not to stoop to dishonesty or immorality.

But soon a crisis came. He fell in love with the wife of a prominent
member of the highest society in the capital. He felt deeply threat-
ened by the whole situation and was in near despair one day over
the struggle to control his passions. That night he dreamed that
he was being accused in a court of some vague crime that he had
perpetrated, though he was aware of being innocent. In order to
escape punishment he swore an oath on the spot that he would

---

eagerly he spoke with Basil's former pupil and protégé, Evagrius, therefore,
since Evagrius would have been in a position to contribute appreciably to the
atmosphere of reverence for the dead Basil which marked the attitude of
Gregory in those years. It was above all doctrinal questions that must have
occupied them since the debates centered about the divinity of the Holy
Spirit.

65. Daniélou, *op. cit.,* 7.

66. This influence of Gregory upon Evagrius has been recognized by I.
Hausherr in his article on Evagrius' work on prayer (*RAM* 15 [1934], 169);
W. Jaeger also has pointed out this influence in *Two Rediscovered Works of
Ancient Christian Literature: Gregory of Nyssa and Macarius* (Leyden, 1954), 208.

67. Festugière, *op. cit.,* 123.

leave Constantinople and "watch after his soul."[68] When he woke
in the morning he gave a good deal of thought to his dream and
decided that "though I was asleep, yet I took the oath."[69] The
next day found him aboard ship, sailing for the Holy Land.

He went straight to Jerusalem. When he arrived there he directed
his steps to the hospice on the Mount of Olives which was operated
for Christian pilgrims by Melania.[70] He was warmly welcomed by
her and invited to stay.

Melania was a Roman lady, wealthy and aristocratic, who had
been widowed. She was living a life of asceticism in a convent
which she had founded near the Mount of Olives not far from the
monastery which her friend Rufinus had founded.[71] She was the
superioress of a group of consecrated virgins, some fifty in number,
and one of their ascetic practices was the caring for pilgrims.

---

68. Budge, *op. cit.,* 341.

69. *Ibid.*

70. Melania was a Roman aristocrat and a wealthy widow since the age of
twenty-two when her husband, Valerius Maximus, the Prefect of Rome, met
an untimely end. She determined to consecrate her life to Christ and to that
purpose set out to study the ascetic life in Egypt in the company of Rufinus.
After meeting some of the more important solitaries in Egypt she went to
Jerusalem where she employed her vast wealth in establishing and supporting
the double monastery on the Mount of Olives, with Rufinus as superior of the
men's community. There is good reason for thinking that Melania was one of
Evagrius' best friends, and even that she clothed him with the monastic habit.
That a lively correspondence continued between her and Evagrius during his
long stay in Egypt is quite clear from the fact that in the Syriac tradition all the
Evagrian letters are stated to be addressed to her (see Muyldermans, *op. cit.,*
76). This is not accurate, of course, but some of the more important data
found in the letters Evagrius wrote are in the letter that is addressed to her and
which is the key to understanding the *Kephalaia Gnostica.* Melania died about
410 AD. For details of her life and family background see F. X. Murphy,
"Melania the Elder: A Biographical Note," *Traditio,* V (1947), 59–77. For
her place in Palestinian monasticism, G. D. Gordini, "Il monachesimo romano
in Palestina nel IV secolo," *St Martin et son Temps,* Studia Anselmiana, 46
(Rome, 1961), 85–107.

71. Rufinus too was to keep in contact with Evagrius in the desert. Indeed
he, Melania and Evagrius formed what Jerome thought of as an unholy trio.
Their friendship included a passionate interest in Origen's theology as well
as a deep attachment to the monastic tradition.

Melania was also a very intelligent and alert woman who read a great deal, especially Origen.[72]

Soon Evagrius had made new friendships in the Holy City. He found both Melania and Rufinus to be more than good hosts; they became dear friends and their friendship would be life-long. Thus things went very smoothly for Evagrius. Indeed, he was so comfortable that before long he had forgotten all about his resolve to dedicate himself to caring for his spiritual welfare. He was becoming once again implicated in worldly ways. "Satan made the heart of Evagrius as hard as the heart of Pharaoh."[73] Then Evagrius fell ill with a fever. The remedies employed by the physicians were unavailing. Melania, however, discovered the true cause of his illness was his conflict over his broken promise and after receiving his confidences about his vocation was able to persuade him to fulfill it by entering a monastic setting. A few days later the fever left him. He "was healed and his whole mind was strengthened."[74]

The next we hear of Evagrius he is settled in Nitria, in the Egyptian desert, with a group of monks. No doubt he had been advised in the matter by Melania who had earlier made a journey through Egypt. She had gone from Alexandria to Nitria where she made friends with some of the more notable monks.

It was no mere accident that the group of monks which Evagrius joined there were Origenists. Melania was devoted to the study of Origen's writings and Rufinus was one of his most ardent disciples. He translated a number of his works into Latin and thus was responsible for propagating Origenist theories in the West. There was a small circle of Origenists in the Jerusalem double monastery with Melania and Rufinus as their leaders. Here Evagrius was initiated into the mysteries of this prolific author while he sojourned at the Jerusalem hospice, though he had some earlier contact with him.

Some scholars have thought that Evagrius was the one who introduced Origenist ideas into the desert. This was not the case. He was the first to write extensively on the spirituality of the desert

72. LH 55:3, p. 136.   73. Budge, *op. cit.,* 342.   74. *Ibid.*

and the first to reduce to a system a monastic ascetic and mystical theology which included many elements of desert wisdom.[75] But when St Epiphanius visited Egypt around 370 he already found Origenists among the more notable of the monks.[76] In view of the proximity of Nitria and other monastic colonies to Alexandria, the site of Origen's early activities, it would be surprising were his ideas to remain unheard of in the desert.

It was around 383 when Evagrius came to Nitria where he was warmly received, doubtless due to a letter which Melania provided. At that moment the chief figures in Nitria were the four Long Brothers (so-called from their extraordinary height). They were the spiritual disciples of the holy monk Pambo whom Melania had visited in 372. Pambo was much taken with Melania (he left her his sole possession when he died: a wicker basket that he had woven that very day!)[77] and so she was held in high esteem by his disciples. At the time of Evagrius' arrival these men were already well known for their lives of asceticism and for their learning. Ammonius Parotes was the leader of the group but before long the community was called the "Group of Ammonius and Evagrius," and a while later simply the "Congregation of Evagrius."[78] Evagrius had become their acknowledged leader and master. He was to maintain this position for the rest of his life.

But Evagrius was not isolated from other groups of monks in the desert. He had close connections with the simple Copts who were quite unacquainted with Origen as with all Hellenistic learning. He became, in fact, a disciple of the Great Macarius, and it remained his practice to visit him from time to time at Scete. Even in his last years when he had a reputation as a writer, Evagrius was proud to refer to himself as a disciple of Macarius.[79]

There was another well-known monk in Egypt called Macarius the Alexandrian. He was a priest of the more austere group of

75. J. Meyendorf, *St Grégoire Palamas et la mystique orthodoxe* (Paris, 1959), 19.

76. St Epiphanius, *Panarion,* ed. G. Dindendorf (Leipzig, 1859), 590.

77. HL 10:5, p. 45.   78. Budge, *op. cit.,* 257.

79. *Praktikos,* final paragraph; also 29.

hermits at Cells.[80] Evagrius also made himself a disciple and friend of this very austere man and continued to visit with him when he himself, after a two year stay in Nitria, decided to move to Cells.[81] He was to live there fourteen years, pursuing a life of prayer and severe asceticism till his premature death in the last year of the fourth century.

It is not easy to learn a great deal about Evagrius from his writings, although he does give hints here and there about more personal matters and at times his personality shows through his austere style. Fortunately there are other sources which give us vivid and sharp pictures of Evagrius at various times of his life in the desert. Not only the work of his disciple Palladius, who devotes a full chapter to him in his *Lausiac History*, and the Syriac version of this history, which incorporates other material, but also a number of apophthegmata, sayings and tales found in the collections of desert wisdom, speak about Evagrius and give us some indications of his way of life during these years.

Palladius tells us that Evagrius led a most austere life, living on small amounts of bread and oil.[82] He underwent the most severe trials against chastity and met them with heroic efforts, such as passing the night exposed to the winter cold standing in a well.[83] His other great trials were those of temptations to blasphemy which seriously tormented him.[84] But he met these too with similarly heroic resistance.

In the meantime he did not neglect his intellectual life. He wrote

80. Cells was a colony of monks some twelve miles south from Nitria, and considered by the monks to have a more austere observance than that of Nitria. Nitria itself is located some forty miles south of Alexandria, consisting of a great valley flanked by two mountain ranges. It had become quite populous since its early beginnings under Amoun in 315. Cells allowed for a more retired life. For further details, see *Dictionnaire d'Archéologie Chrétienne et Liturgie*, 15 (1950), 994–1002: "Scété"; also E. G. E. White, *The Monasteries of the Wâdi Natrûn*, Part II (New York, 1932), 17–36. Recent excavations at Cells give us details of the dwellings there. Cf. A. and C. Guillamont, TP 24, note 1. Cf. also: A. Guillaumont, "Le Cita des 'Cellia,' " *Revue Archéologique*, (1964), Tom II, (July–September), pp. 43–50.

81. LH 38:10, p. 113.   82. *Ibid.*   83. *Ibid.*, 38:11.   84. *Ibid.*

his books[85] and gave spiritual direction for which he soon became well-known by reason of his unusual gifts of "knowledge, and wisdom and the discernment of spirits."[86] These gifts were recognized to be the fruit of his asceticism and purity of heart more than the result of study.[87] Discretion in particular had been considered the essential sign of the true spiritual master since the times of Anthony the Great.[88] In spite of his tendency to express his ideas in strictly formulated definitions and in elaborate and finely articulated systems, Evagrius was considered to possess discretion (which at that time meant especially the discernment of spirits) to a remarkable degree.[89] Stories were told about his verbal battles with the demons in which he came off victorious. In particular he was once assaulted by the demons representing the most destructive heresies of his time: the demon of Arianism, that of Eunomianism and that of Apollinarianism. His gifts were enough to bring him off the victor.[90] He made occasional trips to Alexandria where he engaged heretics in disputation with an equal display of the powers that he received from the Lord.[91] The books that he wrote were intended to deal above all with teaching monks "the cunning of the demons and the snares" of passionate thoughts.[92] But they were not always appreciated and at times caused him considerable grief.

Eucarpius, a defrocked monk and a paragon of arrogance, spoke of Evagrius as a "hewer of words who has led the brethren astray by his writings and caused them to give up their spiritual exercises."[93]

Some of the more personal difficulties Evagrius experienced in adapting himself to the desert life after his brilliant career in Con-

---

85. *Ibid.,* 38:10.   86. *Ibid.*   87. *Ibid.*

88. On the basic importance of discretion in monastic ascetic practice, see R. T. Meyer, *The Life of St Anthony* in ACW, 10 (1950), 57, where we are told that it was above all by his discretion that Anthony so impressed his hearers. For the place of this virtue in fourth-century monasticism in general see P. Resch, *La doctrine ascétique des premiers maîtres égyptiens du quatrième siècle* (Paris, 1931), 95–9.

89. A. J. Festugière, *op. cit.,* 20:15, 123.

90. LH 38:11, pp. 113–14.   91. A. J. Festugière, *op. cit.,* 123.

92. Budge, *op. cit.,* 343.   93. *Ibid.,* 406.

stantinople are preserved in the Syriac tradition. They give some concrete picture of the nature of his struggles as well as indicating the ideas that his fellow-monks and later generations of Christians formed of him. There is the story about Evagrius' trip to Scete to visit a certain Desert Father (probably Macarius the Great) to ask him the customary question: " 'Tell me some piece of advice by which I might be able to save my soul.' The old man answered him: 'If you wish to save your soul do not speak before you are asked a question.' Now this bit of advice was very disturbing to Evagrius and he displayed some chagrin at having asked it for he thought: 'Indeed, I have read many books and I cannot accept instruction of this kind.' Having derived much profit from his visit he left the old man."[94]

There is another story which makes it quite clear that Evagrius did not take readily to the desert concept of humility and silence, and that this difficulty of his was not hidden from his Coptic brethren who, doubtless, had a sharp eye for the shortcomings of the cultured Greek living in their midst. On a certain occasion when the Council of Elders of Cells was in session discussing problems of interest to the community Evagrius came forth with his own views "and an elder said to him: 'We know, Abba, that if you had remained in your own country where you are a bishop (*sic*) and the governor of many [your speech would have been quite in order]; but in this place you sit as a stranger.' Evagrius was chagrined but he did not take offense. He just shook his head and looked down to the ground and wrote with his finger and told them: 'You are right my fathers: I have spoken once. But I will not do so a second time.' "[95] The political overtones of this passage are obvious; the fact that Evagrius was Greek and connected in high places at the Byzantine Court did nothing to make his life easier among the simple Egyptian fellahs become monks. Another interesting bit of information contained in this passage is the evidence it provides for the influence of the traditional desert spirituality upon Evagrius. He accepts their advice, whereas his

94. *Ibid.*, 606.
95. *Ibid.*, 606–7. The scriptural reference here is to Job 40:5.

own is rejected. He was as much a disciple of the desert fathers as he was a student of Origen, and this is nowhere more evident than in these two stories.

Evagrius was seen not only as a gifted writer and strenuous ascetic but also as a lovable master. He gathered disciples about him by virtue of his spiritual powers and because of his human qualities. As he grew in purity of heart and attained to the high degree of self-control that is the prerequisite for contemplation, he also grew in charity. There is another tale preserved only in the Syriac tradition which gives us much light on this side of Evagrius' character.

Evagrius went to Alexandria with a group of monks on a business trip. While walking along in the city they came upon a renegade monk who had deserted the monastic life to take up his lot with the low life of the metropolis. In fact he was actually speaking with a street-walker when Evagrius came upon him. Immediately Evagrius approached him with the greatest signs of respect and friendliness, though he could not refrain from weeping at the sight of such depravity in a former monk. He managed to persuade the man, Stephana by name, to lodge with him and the other monks while they were in the city. When he entered their lodgings Evagrius affectionately embraced him and pleaded with him to return to the desert, assuring him with the most touching kindness of the mercy of God. But his trouble was for nothing. Stephana had nothing but contempt and mockery to utter for monks and their ways. "And the blessed Evagrius and the brethren wept and groaned over him greatly."[96]

As Evagrius' reputation for holiness and his abilities became known the Patriarch of Egypt, Theophilus of Alexandria, became interested in him. He wished to ordain him bishop of Thmuis.[97] Evagrius, however, firmly resisted. He knew that if a monk was to remain faithful to his calling he had to follow the advice of the Fathers who had taught that monks must "avoid women and

---

96. *Ibid.*, 402.
97. Socrates, *Historia ecclesiastica* 4:23; PG 67:521B.

bishops."[98] He continued in the way of humility and supported himself by copying books.[99] Evagrius' last years were marked by deep peace and the increase of his spiritual powers. He came to be referred to as "that man of understanding,"[100] and he had a reputation for working miracles as well as for the gift of prophecy.[101] During the last three years of his life, he is said to have confided to the brethren, he had attained such a degree of *apatheia* that he was no longer troubled by disordered passions and thoughts.[102]

His health had begun to fail the last years of his life but he made little change in his austere regimen. He only allowed himself the use of cooked food to replace the raw vegetables he was accustomed to when his stomach could no longer digest the rougher fare.[103] In his Letter to Anatolius he mentions his illness, though he is not specific as to the precise nature of it.

The end came prematurely. He was fifty-five when he sensed that he was at the verge of death. The year was 399, and it was the Feast of the Epiphany, the Feast of the Light of Christ revealed to the believing Gentiles. The last thing we learn of Evagrius was that he asked to be taken to the church for the Feast so that he could participate in the mysteries.[104] He received Holy Communion there and died peacefully in the Lord.

98. This "beware of bishops" so as to avoid all occasion of either ambition or of involvement in distracting cares through being ordained a priest became a kind of standing pleasantry among the Fathers of the Desert, as one may observe from the banter between Palladius and John of Lycopolis. LH 35:10–11, p. 101f.

99. LH 38:10, p. 113. L. Duchesne observes that the art of calligraphy was practiced in Nitria as a form of work by certain of the more cultivated monks (*Histoire ancienne de l'Église,* 2 [1911], 497). Palladius tells us that Evagrius was quite skilled in this work and that he made use of the oxyrhynchus characters. Indeed, some scholars have thought that the beautiful ms H of St Paul's epistles was copied by Evagrius' own hand, on the basis of a signature found on the ms. (Thus Armitage-Robinson in C. Butler, *The Lausiac History of Palladius* [Cambridge, 1898] 1, 3, 6; R. Devresse, *Introduction à l'étude des manuscrits grecs* (Paris, 1954), 23 and 163, also discusses and favors this view.) It remains dubious, however, since the name "Evagrius" that is thought to appear on this ms as the scribe is not the correct reading.

100. Budge, *op. cit.,* 1043.   101. LH 38:12, p. 114.

102. *Ibid.,* 38:13.   103. *Ibid.*   104. *Ibid.*

He did not realize it but his early death spared him a trial greater than any he had been subjected to in his lifetime. Before the same year had ended his followers were being persecuted as heretics by their Metropolitan, the Patriarch Theophilus, Evagrius' former admirer. The charge was Origenism.

THE HISTORY OF EVAGRIAN THEOLOGY

Origenism

The struggles centering about the Origenist heresy were to plague the Church in Egypt, Palestine and Constantinople for many years to come. This is not the place to attempt to unravel all the complex history of this painful episode in the annals of early monasticism.[105] Let us simply state that the trouble had been threatening for some years, ever since Epiphanius had complained in his *Panarion* in 374 of the presence of Origenists in Nitria.[106]

Trouble came more from the Coptic monks than from Epiphanius. Naturally they would view with suspicion the intellectual pursuits of the more cultured and refined monks of Hellenistic background. At least the less spiritual-minded and less intelligent among them felt some such hesitations about accepting the presence of men whose type of spirituality seemed to them to threaten their own traditions. One of their chief objections to the system taught by Evagrius was the immateriality of God, the doctrine that held he was pure spirit. This was indeed a key-stone in the Evagrian system. Literally all depended upon it. In opposition to this view the Copts for the most part held an anthropomorphic concept of the divinity. They considered that he was in his very form a pattern for the structure of the human body, except in larger proportions. After all, they reasoned, the Bible tells us that man is made in the image and likeness of God.[107]

---

105. For a good detailed account of this history see Guillaumont, 81–166.

106. Epiphanius, *Panarion*, 64:4, ed. G. Dindendorf (Leipzig, 1859), 590.

107. Guillaumont, 61. This author has a very interesting discussion of the origins of this anthropomorphite theology. He sees it as a development taking

Probably it was the very success of Evagrius' teaching, among other factors, which prompted them to press the Patriarch for a decision in this matter. He put them off at first with considerable diplomatic skill. The Copts knew of Theophilus' former favorable attitude to the Origenists—had he not wanted to make Evagrius himself a bishop? So they were suspicious of his motives in hesitating to condemn their erring brethren. They would not be put off, and indicated it with the very forceful methods which came quite naturally to a large crowd of angry and fanatical men determined to win what they considered their rights. Theophilus saw that he was defeated. He was not the man to suffer the loss of all things for a principle. He determined to condemn Origenism and to that end convoked a synod of bishops at Alexandria where he induced them to produce the required condemnation.

When the followers of Evagrius refused to acquiesce in this decision and offered resistance to the measures taken to suppress them, the Patriarch employed troops to quell their rebellion. In a short time they were forced into exile. Among those who fled were some of the most renowned among the ascetics of the desert: the four Long Brothers, Palladius, John Cassian and his companion Germanus. All these latter eventually found refuge with John Chrysostom who was at that moment the Patriarch of Constantinople. Before the entire episode was complete Chrysostom himself would die in exile.[108]

Thus did the Community of Evagrius come to an abrupt and violent end. In the event, however, this proved to be the end only of the Egyptian phase of its history. With the departure of the emigrés a new period of its life began, one which would carry the work of Evagrius and his followers to all parts of the Christian

---

place in reaction to the mystical theology of the *Chapters on Prayer* of Evagrius, notably the view that one goes "immaterial to the Immaterial" (see c. 66), This struck the more earthy Copts as being too spiritualized a concept of God.

108. For further details of the condemnation and the subsequent events see Guillaumont, 63f.

D

world and hand it down the centuries to the future. Evagrius' teaching found eloquent spokesmen in the persons of Palladius and Cassian, both of whose writings achieved wide and enduring renown.

But it was not to be transplanted full grown, root and branch. John Cassian in particular was to interpret Evagrius' doctrine to the Latin world. He understood that it was necessary to prune away the coarse excretions of an over-severity that was ill suited to the more temperate climate of his native France.[109] In the process he created a more supple form of life. This new growth remained essentially the same stock as the Nitrian asceticism of Evagrius with its orientation to purity of heart and its culmination in the state of pure prayer. But in the transplanting it grew more verdant and fresh with the bloom of a milder spring. In a short time it was found as suited to the Gallic landscape as ever any native growth might be.[110]

This same process of transplanting and transformation would be repeated in different ways and under diversified forms throughout the Roman Empire. Before long it would carry the teachings of Evagrius through Syria and the mountainous regions of Armenia and far into Persia where it was vastly influential. Eventually even the Arabic world would not only welcome his works into its literature but even pass them on to the Ethiopian Church which proved to be eager to collect and translate his works.[111]

109. J. Cassian, *Institutions Cénobitiques,* Preface, 9; ed. J. P. Guy, SC 109 (1965), 32f.

110. St John Chrysostom, who had ordained Cassian a deacon, exercised a moderating influence upon his presentation of the Evagrian system of spirituality, although Chrysostom himself was favorable to the circle of Evagrius' followers. There is, further, evidence that Cassian and Chrysostom share common sources for certain aspects of their teaching.

111. O. Spies, "Die äthiopische Uberlieferung der Abhandlung des Evagrius," *Oriens Christianus,* 7–3F (1932), 203. The author points out the large number of mss. of the treatise he edits here as one of the clear indications of the popularity of Evagrius in the Church of Ethopia. Surprisingly, the Arabic text was used as basis for the translation into Ethopian, which was made about 1551 AD.

Above all it was the Syrian Church which gave the most sympathetic hearing to the doctrines of Evagrius. All his major writings were translated into the Syriac tongue very early,[112] and soon after passed on by this church to the Armenians who translated them into their own tongue. The result was that the teachings of Evagrius have played a major role in the ascetic and mystical theology of the Syriac tradition. Not only were they copied in large numbers and widely circulated, but important commentaries were written on his works by some of the outstanding Syrian theologians.[113] One of the reasons for this was that the Syriac world was left largely untroubled by the Origenist and Pelagian conflicts. But perhaps the more important reason is that the writings of this ardent monk with his concentration on a severe asceticism and the complete orientation of life to mystical prayer appealed to the temper of the Syriac world, more Oriental than classical in its tendencies.

In the Latin world the reception of Evagrius was at first enthusiastic on the part of large numbers. The translations of Rufinus had a wide audience and so popularized Evagrius that even the strictures of St Jerome, as severe as they were,[114] could not prevent the

112. There are a number of Syriac mss. which are appreciably earlier than any of the Greek mss. which are extant. Some date to the sixth century. In addition some of the works of Evagrius are found in several distinct translations and for that reason have a special value in establishing the critical text. See Muyldermans, *op. cit.*, 6 and 31.

113. Guillaumont, 19, referring to the commentary of Babai the Great, quotes "Evagrius' work became the chief manual and the authoritative exposition of the ascetico-mystical way of life for Persian monasticism."— Cyprian Rice, *The Persian Sufis* (London, 1964), 22. It was Babai the Great, abbot of the monastery of Mt Izla in Persia, who introduced Evagrius' works so successfully into Persia that they continued to be active even after the Moslem conquest, and have decisively influenced the development of the spirituality of the Persian Sufis.

114. See the *Epistle to Ctesiphon*, 133:3; PL 22:1151A. St Jerome considered Evagrius and the Origenists generally to be the precursors of the Pelagians. Cavallera considers that he did this "quite artificially" and that this view is untenable (F. Cavallera, *St Jerôme: Sa vie et son oeuvre*, 2 (Paris, 1922), 125. But a recent author takes the opposite side of the argument (J. Gross, *Entstehungsgeschichte des Erbsündendogmas* (Munich, 1963), 163, as cited by F. Refoulé, *op. cit.*, 223).

continuing influence of Evagrius. In addition to the spread of his teachings by the Latin translation of his works by Rufinus, and later a second translation by Gennadius, there was the personal influence of the exiled Origenists who turned to the Latin West. Above all, the writings of Cassian assured the ideas of Evagrius wide welcome in the spirituality of the Benedictine monasteries. St Benedict named Cassian along with St Basil as Fathers whose writings he most highly recommended to his monks.[115] His recommendation was taken very seriously as the great popularity of both of Cassian's major works in the Benedictine centuries attests.[116] Besides these books there were the many translations of Palladius' History[117] which not only speaks about Evagrius but illustrates his ascetic and mystical teaching.

When the Fifth Ecumenical Council condemned the Origenism of Evagrius there was a marked reaction against propagating his writings. The immediate occasion of this condemnation was the revival of interest in Origenistic and Evagrian spirituality on the part of a group of fervent Palestinian monks living in the New Lavra. This group was opposed by the higoumenos of the Great Lavra, Gelasius. Political interests led to involvement on the part of the Basileus and violent scenes characterized the struggle. In the face of this threat to orthodoxy and to unity Justinian insisted on the Council's giving a decision on the question.

The Council issued a statement containing fifteen anathemas against Origenism.[118] The Origenists at the New Lavra, however, would not accept the decree.[119] They were forcefully expelled and

---

115. *The Rule of St Benedict,* trans. J. McCann (London, 1952), 160. c. 73, ed., G. Penco (Firenze, 1970), p. 188.

116. Both the *Institutes* and the *Conferences* of Cassian have been among the most popular monastic spiritual reading down through the centuries. St Benedict recommends both of these works. Cassian's third major piece of writing, *De Incarnatione,* was much less popular. It is a dogmatic treatise.

117. For a detailed discussion of some of the problems arising from this fact, LH, p. 9.

118. Guillaumont, 133ff.   119. *Ibid.,* 136.

replacements from the Great Lavra were sent to repopulate the monastery. This final measure spelled the end of the Origenists as a force in history. The condemnation pronounced by the Ecumenical Council was the reason for the eclipse of Evagrius' work. The reaction set in immediately both in the East and the West.

Later History of Evagrian Writings

In spite of the eclipse his name suffered Evagrius continued to exercise a vast influence upon the spirituality of the Church in many cultures and in various ways. One of the reasons for this is that many persons thought a great deal of the usefulness of his writings. Not all of them were intellectuals. Both of the works translated in this volume had wide appeal, especially for monks but also for Christians of all classes who read them for centuries without discovering in them anything harmful to orthodox faith.[120] The *Chapters on Prayer* were preserved by passing under the name of the respected St Nilus.[121] A few other works were also preserved in the original Greek even though they were known to be works of Evagrius.[122]

One of the interesting ways in which Evagrius managed to continue to teach in his native tongue was through the translation

---

120. I. Hausherr has stressed this in *Les Leçons d'une Contemplative* (Paris, 1960), 7–8. One of the arguments against Evagrius is the lack of references to the name of Jesus or his person and to the sacraments in his work on prayer. Yet, while this has some significance, too much weight must not be put on it, for other works of antiquity, even by some great Fathers, display certain serious lacunae. E.g., B. Steidle, *Die Regel St Benedikts* (Beuron, 1952), 189ff. has pointed to the paucity of sacramental theology in the Benedictine spirituality. The recently published second part of the *Letter to Melania*, moreover, places the person of Jesus at the center of Evagrius' thought.

121. There were others too whose name lent shelter to some of Evagrius' works, Gregory of Nazianzen and St Basil being the two most renowned.

122. Other works in Greek are the *Sentences for Monks*, *The Exhortation to a Virgin*, the *Praktikos* and the *Hypotyposis*, to name the more important ones.

into Greek of the works of Isaac the Syrian.[123] This great theologian
of the mystical life was profoundly indebted to Evagrius for much
of his teaching, so that when his works were put into Greek to a
great extent Evagrius was readmitted into his mother Church,
though like Isaac of old she did not recognize his identity: "The
voice is the voice of Jacob, but the hands are the hands of Esau."[121]

It is clear that some of the greatest Byzantine writers had studied
Evagrius very thoroughly and had incorporated his basic concepts
of the spiritual life in varying degree into their systems of ascetic

123. Isaac the Syrian, also known as Isaac of Nineveh (died about 700), is an
important spiritual author of the Syrian Church. Originally a monk of
Bethabe in Kurdistan he became the Nestorian bishop of Nineveh. But he
soon returned to become a hermit, then finally a monk in the monastery of
Rabban Shapur in the mountains of Persia. His literary remains are very
considerable and much appreciated by the Syrian Church. But they remain
almost wholly unpublished in Syriac, though translations in several other
languages are printed. He is often confused with Isaac of Antioch, who lived
in the fourth century, and one of the difficulties about editing his work is the
confusion of the mss. tradition. For bibliography see, *Oxford Dictionary of the
Christian Church*, ed. F. L. Cross (London, 1963): "Isaac of Nineveh," 703.
For further evidence of Evagrian influence on Nestorians see E. A. W. Budge,
The Book of Governors, 2 vols. (London, 1893), *passim*. The recent edition of the
Asceticon of Abba Isaiah of Scete adds another page to the textual history and
to the influence of Evagrius in the Syriac world. See R. Draguet, *Les Cinq
Recensions de l'Asceticon Syriac d'Abba Isaie* (Louvain, 1968), vol. 1, 10.
Scattered throughout this work are references to Evagrius which provide
certain data for situating him in the monastic tradition as well as evaluating
his influence.

124. Gen 27:22.

125. Viller, *passim,* and Völker, 490.

126. Diadoch of Photicus is a figure about whom very little is known beyond that he was the bishop of Photicus and that he attended the Council of
Chalcedon. He has written some very interesting spiritual reflections which,
while influenced by Evagrius, of themselves contribute to the development of
the Byzantine mystical and ascetic theology. Bouyer, *op. cit.,* 430ff. has a
good study of his doctrine, and his works have been published recently. Ed.
E. des Places, *Oeuvres Spirituelles de Diadoque de Photice,* SC 5 bis (1955).

127. St John Climachus, though a very original writer as his *Ladder of
Divine Ascent* clearly indicates, is essentially a disciple of Evagrius as regards
his basic conception of the relations between asceticism and contemplation
(see H. G. Beck, *Kirche und Theologische Literatur im Byzantinischen Reich*
[Munich, 1959], 353f.). W. Völker, in his recent study of Climachus, shows
that it is that part of Evagrius which is rooted in the Apophthegmata and

and mystical theology. In recent times it has been possible to trace out a good deal of the course traveled by Evagrian theology through the centuries. Besides the considerable influence he had upon Maximus the Confessor,[125] Evagrius contributed to the theology of Diadoch of Photicus,[126] St John Climachus,[127] Hesychius,[128] Nicetas Stethatos,[129] and Symeon the New Theologian.[130] His theology also came to be important in the hesychastic school of spirituality through being incorporated in the teaching of Gregory of Sinai[131] who in some sense can be called the originator of the movement which culminated in the works of Gregory

which was accepted by Barsanuphius as safe and valuable which has influenced Climachus. See his *Scala Paradisi* (Wiesbaden, 1968) v, vi, 7. This applies in particular to his studies of the chief vices. *Ibid.,* 69ff. But he did not always take kindly to Evagrius, going so far as to call him "cursed" (*The Ladder of Divine Ascent,* trans. L. Moore [New York, 1960], 141). Climachus is still the most influential of writers on monastic matters among the Russian monks. Indeed, it has been recently pointed out that his work has played a part in the formation of the character of modern Russia, notably through Dostoyevsky. See T. Merton, *Disputed Questions* (New York, 1960), 88.

128. Hesychius was the abbot of the Monastery of the Thornbush on Mt Sinai, and lived probably in the seventh century. His two *Centuries* represent a blending of elements taken from Evagrius and Climachus into an original synthesis that marked another stage in the development of Byzantine spirituality. These works are printed in PG 93:1480–1544, where they are erroneously ascribed to Hesychius of Jerusalem. See Beck, *op. cit., supra* note 127, 453.

129. Nicetas Stethatos was an important figure in the Byzantine world at the time of the Great Schism in the mid-eleventh century. Born in 1020, he entered the Studite Monastery at the age of fourteen and soon became the favorite disciple of Symeon the New Theologian who was living there at the time. Later he wrote the life of Symeon and also edited his works. In addition he wrote a number of books himself. He died about 1090. For further details of his life and a recent edition of his works, *Nicetas Stethatos: Opuscules et Lettres,* ed. A. Darrouzès, SC 81 (Paris, 1961).

130. Symeon the New Theologian represents the high-point of the post-patristic mystical theology of the Byzantine tradition. He fills out the Evagrian framework, which he basically accepts, with the more affective emphasis of Diadoch and of pseudo-Macarius. But his own mystical experience and the strongly personal style put a highly distinctive mark on all that he wrote. See the discussion in Beck, 360ff. and 585 for further particulars, and more especially *Symeon le Nouveau Theologien: Catéchèse,* ed. B. Krivocheine, SC, 96, vol. 1 (Paris, 1963), the Introduction.

131. Gregory of Sinai, born towards the end of the thirteenth century, became a monk first on the island of Cyprus, but before long transferred to

Palamas.[132] The spiritual descendants of Palamas, such as the compilers of the *Philokalia,* Nikodemus and Macarius,[133] as well as the important group of Orthodox theologians of our own time who have been referred to as the Neo-palamites[134]—all are in varying degree influenced by the Evagrian point of view. In fact it is the Russian Orthodox who have come to be more devoted to the spiritual theology of the *Philokalia* (in Russian, the *Dobrotolyubie*)[135] than any of the other churches. One of the major pieces contained in this collection of writings is the One Hundred Chapters of the *Praktikos* by Evagrius.[136] The extent to which the spirit of the

---

Mt Sinai where he made a number of disciples. He soon had to leave there, however, and settled on Crete where he encountered an elderly monk who introduced him to the practices of hesychasm, the contemplatively oriented monastic observance. When later on he moved to Mt Athos he found scarcely one there who practiced the hesychastic observance and so he set about to establish it there himself and thus gave rise to the movement which was to culminate in the experience and writings of the influential Gregory Palamas not long after Gregory's death in 1346. For particulars of his teaching, see Beck, *op. cit., supra* note 127, 694-5.

132. Gregory Palamas, born in Constantinople about 1296, is easily one of the most influential of the Byzantine theologians and mystics. After he had dedicated himself to his studies—with the significant exclusion of philosophy— he was introduced into mysticism by Theoleptus of Philadelpia. He then entered the Athos monastic community and became a disciple of Gregory of Sinai. An invasion by the Turks caused him to flee from there after five years and this led to his founding a new monastery in Macedonia, near Berrhoia, with a group of like-minded monks. The incursions of Serbs forced him to return to Athos. An important controversy with Barlaam broke out at this time and occupied a great deal of his activity and gave him great prominence. He wrote mystical treatises in addition to controversial works and was accorded official recognition, so that even in his life time his theology became the recognized property of Mt Athos. He died in 1359 and was beatified by the Patriarch Philotheos in 1368. See Beck, *op. cit., supra* note 127, 712ff. for a more thorough discussion.

133. For a brief account of Nikodemus the Hagiorite and Macarius of Corinth see the article by Un Moine de l'Eglise d'Orient. "La Prière de Jésus," *Irénikon.* 20 (1947). 391ff.

134. This term is used by E. von Ivánka, "Palamismus und Vätertradition," *L'Eglise et les eglises,* 2 (Chevtogne, 1955), 41. This group of young and very influential theologians have reinterpreted the Palamite theology for our own times in the conviction that it is a basic element of the Byzantine tradition and still valid for our times. According to Ivánka their way of interpreting

Dobrotolyubie penetrated into the soul of nineteenth-century Russia is best illustrated by the moving and beautiful story of the Russian peasant whose one aim was to follow the prescriptions of its teaching.[137]

Pseudo-Denis, the Areopagite, who was perhaps more influential in the West than in the East, though he had a considerable number of followers in Byzantium, is now known to have borrowed some of the basic elements of his own theological system from Evagrius.[138] Through him Evagrian teachings penetrated deeply into the mystical writers of the Middle Ages in the West.[139]

Palamas presents no difficulty to the traditional view of the simple nature of the Divinity, although the teaching of Palamas himself did present such a difficulty. It should be noted that in the spirituality of the Byzantine world, including the Russian Orthodox, the Palamite theology has been predominant, at the expense of those writers whose teaching tends to stress other elements of spirituality than the contemplative. For instance such great spiritual writers as Basil the Great, Barsanuphius, Dorotheus and Theodore the Studite are all excluded from the *Philokalia*. See the discussion by J. Meyendorf, *St Gregoire Palamas et la mystique orthodoxe* (Paris, 1959), 174–78 on hesychastic tradition.

135. This Russian translation, with the considerable additions it incorporates, has played a prominent role in the Orthodox Russian spirituality. That it continues to do so is evidenced by the fact that a new printing is being undertaken at present by the monks of Holy Trinity monastery: *Dobrotolyubie,* 5 vols (Jordanville, N.Y., 1963). It is a reprint of the 2nd ed. (Mt Athos, 1883). It has been partly translated into English: *Early Fathers from the Philokalia,* trans. E. Kadloubovsky and G. Palmer (London, 1959) and the companion volume by the same translators, *Writings from the Philokalia on Prayer of the Heart* (London, 1959).

136. *Dobrotolyubie,* 1 (Jordanville, N.Y., 1963) 421–36.

137. *The Way of a Pilgrim,* trans. R. M. French (New York, 1952). The pilgrim actually must have used the Slavonic translation, made by Paissy Velichkovsky (Moscow, 1793) since the Russian translation was made only in 1877 by Theophane the Recluse. There is an interesting piece of evidence for the fact that Evagrius was read by the pilgrim, for on p. 76 we read: "When the spirit prays purely without being led astray then the demons no longer come upon it from the left side but from the right." Cf. *Chapters on Prayer,* 72. Actually it is the staretz who speaks these words to the pilgrim, but he has so completely assimilated them that they belong as completely to him as to Evagrius.

138. Bouyer, *op. cit.,* 399–400, 413 and 421.

139. See the informative article by A. Rayez, M. A. Fracheboud *et al.,* in D.S., 3:318–429: "Denys l'Areopagite," which discusses the extensive in-

It is not clear how far the writings of Evagrius had a direct influence upon certain mystics of the West, such as John of the Cross[140] and Ruysbroeck,[141] but there are reasons for thinking they had some knowledge of his theology by writings other than those of Pseudo-Denis.

Nearly all the writers mentioned in this long list of saints and theologians derived such parts of their doctrine as were taken from the teachings of Evagrius largely from the two works here translated. They contain the essence of his ascetico-mystical system in its relation to the life of prayer. In spite of the heretical elements[142] in his speculative theology and the tendencies to extremism which are to be found in certain passages in Evagrius' writings, there pulses the life that is a longing for God and which is a sign of the

---

fluence upon the western mystics and theologians of Pseudo-Denis. The list of his disciples includes some of the greatest saints and doctors of the Roman Church: St Albert the Great, St Thomas Aquinas, Eckhardt, Fenélon, etc. To obtain an impression of the depth and the power of this influence one has only to read the extensive commentary of St Thomas on the *Divine Names*.

140. Hausherr, *Leçons,* 19. Also the very provocative article, "Les Orientaux connaissent-ils les 'nuits' de Saint Jean de la Croix?" *OCP*, 12 (1946), 5–46.

141. Jan van Ruysbroeck (1293–1381) is one of the greatest mystics of the West. He lived as a canon regular of St Augustine in a hermitage near Brussels and wrote a number of important works dealing with the mystical life. He is the head of the school of *devotio moderna.* That he may well have read some of Evagrius is a conclusion one is inclined to draw after perusing some of his work, for instance chapter twelve of his *Book of Supreme Truth* where he refers to *bare images,* the *divine brightness,* conformity of the *created* image with the *uncreated* image through *contemplation.* See this passage in J. E. Sullivan, *The Image of God* (Dubuque, 1964), 291–2, note 200.

142. It is useful to point out here that for many of the churches Evagrius was never considered a heretic. On the contrary he has been venerated as one of the great saints by several of them, above all the Jacobite Syrians honor him as one of the first among their holy doctors. Indeed, John Bar Kaldoun lists him ahead of St Basil, St Chrysostom and others. Isaac of Nineveh speaks of him as the "greatest of contemplatives," and in the Syrian martyrology of Raban Sliba (*Analecta Bollandia,* 27 [1908], 173) Evagrius has a commemoration for January 16th. The Nestorians commemorate him in the Canon of the Mass and the Copts celebrate his feast on the Fifth Sunday of Lent, while the Armenians have his feast on the 11th of February. See Guillaumont, 198–9. The Georgian Church, which considers Evagrius a native son, holds him in the highest honor and considers him its first monk. See M. Tarchnisvili, p. 307, *op. cit.*

Spirit who is himself the living tradition of the Church.[143] It is the presence of this Spirit which is the reason for the wide and enduring influence of this monk and writer upon the spiritual life of the Church, especially through the *Praktikos* and the *Chapters on Prayer.*

THE WRITINGS

The list of Evagrian writings is an extensive one. Establishing the precise number and names of all his works is a task beset with certain serious difficulties. As we have already seen, considerable ingenuity was needed to preserve some of his works from the fire. This meant using pseudo-authors on the title page at times. However, there is considerable agreement on a good deal of the Evagrian corpus and it is possible to give a rather detailed statement as to the state of the research into this matter at present.

Certainly Authentic Works

1. *The Praktikos*

One of the two works translated in this volume, the *Praktikos* deals with the ascetic life but actually has a good deal about prayer as well as about the work of cleansing the affections of passionate and disordered impulses. It was one of Evagrius' most popular works. Even today manuscripts containing this work are found in libraries of the East and West alike. This very fact of the number of manuscripts preserved and their broad distribution has prevented the establishing of a critical edition up to the present.[144] It is the best

---

143. V. Lossky and L. Ouspensky, *The Meaning of Ikons* (Boston, 1952), 17–18.

144. See ES, 26-27. While this work was in galleys, the critical edition was published, and we have been able to refer to it. It is excellent. Cf. below, note 34, p. 11.

preserved text of the entire corpus of the Greek Evagriana.[145] It is also found in Syriac and Armenian versions.

Although it is an independent whole in itself yet it forms a trilogy as Evagrius himself tells us,[146] the *Gnostikos* and the *Kephalaia Gnostica* being its two companion pieces.

2. *The Gnostikos*

Within the trilogy mentioned above, the *Praktikos* and the *Gnostikos* formed a special unit and were known together as the *Monachikos*.[147] The *Gnostikos* has but fifty chapters or sentences in contrast with the hundred chapters of the *Praktikos*. It has been transmitted only in the Syriac and Armenian translations, although a number of fragments of considerable interest have been preserved in the original Greek.[148] The *Gnostikos* is written for contemplatives rather than for those concentrating primarily on the ascetic life. But it concentrates on practical advice for this group of monks rather than on speculation.

3. *Kephalaia Gnostica* (Problemata Gnostica)

This is Evagrius' major speculative treatise. It is a kind of *Summa Theologica* of his cosmological and anthropological thought and contains a great deal of philosophical material. It is above all in this work that the ideas for which he was condemned are to be found.

This work consists of six Centuries of aphoristic sayings. Curiously, the Centuries contain only ninety such sentences or chapters rather than the expected hundred. There is a collection of sixty sentences which is known as the *Supplement* for the reason that it brings the number up to six hundred for the six Centuries. It seems to be preserved only in a single Syriac manuscript.[149] There is

---

145. *Ibid.*, 26.   146. *Letter to Anatolius,* below, p. 15.

147. Socrates, *Historia ecclesiastica,* 3:7; PG 67:516A.

148. See the interesting fragment printed in PG 40:1285, preserved by Socrates in his history (c. 4:23).

149. In the Vatican Syr 178. See ES, 66.

some question as to whether the *Supplement* was actually prepared by Evagrius himself.[150]

This work has been almost completely lost in the original Greek, and even the "received text" of the Syriac version was a skillful re-writing of a good deal of the material so as to produce a text which was free of objectionable doctrines for the most part though not entirely.[151] It has been edited by Frankenberg, though somewhat carelessly, with a retro-version into the original Greek.[152]

There is a second Syriac translation which preserves the original text very closely that has recently been discovered and published. This version allows a more accurate and complete evaluation of Evagrian theology than has hitherto been possible.[153] It reveals clearly the justice of the condemnation of the Christology of this work.[154]

4. *The Chapters on Prayer*

This work is the most important of all the Evagrian corpus. It is here translated into English for the first time. It is preserved in the Greek under the name of St Nilus of Sinai. It was always ascribed to Evagrius by the Syrians and Armenians, and Hausherr has proved they were correct in doing so.[155] Although the entire text was probably translated into Syriac at one time[156] only a part of it is preserved in that tongue.[157] The work consists of a Prologue in the form of a letter and 153 sentences on prayer.

---

150. *Ibid.* 151. Guillaumont, 256–57.

152. Frankenberg, *Evagrius Pontikos* (Berlin, 1912).

153. This is the version discovered by Guillaumont in 1952 and published in PO 28:1.

154. Guillaumont, 159, and also F. Refoulé, *op. cit.,* 251ff.

155. I. Hausherr, "Le traité de l'oraison d'Evagre le Pontique," *RAM*, 15 (1934), 169. This is now generally accepted: see ES, 39, note 67.

156. I. Hausherr, "Le *De Oratione* d'Evagre le Pontique en syriaque et en arabe," *OCP*, 5 (1939), 69.

157. That is the first thirty-five chapters in Syriac. They correspond to the first thirty-two chapters of the Greek text. ES, 39.

5. *Antirrheticos.*

This work is one that is entirely characteristic of Evagrius in his traditional side, that is to say it reflects the part of his teaching which he took over almost exclusively from the Bible and the desert tradition and reworked in his own very distinctive manner. It deals with the eight kinds of passionate thoughts. Evagrius was the first to draw up the catalogue of these and to fill out the description of them. In this work Evagrius cites a series of scriptural texts in their proper order from Genesis to the Apocalypse which can be useful in the fight against these evil tendencies and thoughts. It contains some 487 citations in all,[158] each division of the work having the passages appropriate to the particular *logismos* that is its theme. It is one of the much appreciated works of Evagrius. It exists only in the Syriac and Armenian. The Latin translation made by Gennadius[159] has perished.

6. *Sentences for Monks*

In distinct contrast with all the preceding works this treatise is intended primarily for cenobites. Evagrius usually had hermits in mind when he wrote. This book has been edited in the original Greek version by Gressman,[160] but the Syriac text remains unedited. It is also published in the Armenian edition of his works and there is a Latin version in Migne.[161] Wilmart has pointed out how influential this work was in the West in the fifth and sixth centuries.[162]

---

158. See the description in A. and C. Guillaumont, DS 4:1734 (1960): "Evagre le Pontique."

159. Gennadius, *De vir. ill.,* 11 (PL 58:1066); he describes the work at some length and remarks that he was careful to preserve the original simplicity that characterizes this most biblical of works.

160. H. Gressman, *Nonnenspiegel und Mönchsspiegel des Euagrios Pontikos* (Leipzig, 1913). Muyldermans, *op. cit.,* 29, discusses the edition of Gressman and states the position of the Syriac text in the tradition.

161. PG 40:1277–83.

162. A. Wilmart, *op. cit.,* 152.

7. *Exhortation to a Virgin.*

This work too has been preserved in the Greek original and edited by Gressman.[163] It has been preserved too in Syriac and Armenian and Wilmart has published a Latin translation[164] which is quite distinct from the one printed in Holstenius. This work is preserved in only a very few manuscripts, differing in this from the *Sentences for Monks* for which we have numerous copies.

8. *Hypotyposis.*

The *Hypotyposis* or *Principles of the Monastic Life,* describes the obligatory practices of those who become monks. It concentrates especially on the need for *hesychia* or recollection and the way of life required to maintain a more or less constant state of spiritual concentration. This work is preserved in Greek also and is included in the *Philokalia.*[165] It is also extant in Syriac and Armenian translations. Indeed there are three distinct Syriac translations.[166]

Guillaumont[167] has some doubts about the Evagrian authorship of this work, largely on the basis of the style which lacks the originality and freshness that is usually found in Evagrius. But the manuscript tradition is constant in its attribution, although one passage of this work is found among the works of Ammonas.[168]

9. *Treatise to the Monk Eulogius.*[169]

Although some of the Greek manuscripts ascribe this work to Evagrius some doubt could well be entertained as to the authenticity of this work since the majority of the Greek manuscripts attribute it to St Nilus. Indeed Guillaumont considers it a doubtfully genuine work in spite of the fact that the Armenian and especially the Syriac tradition which has a large number of extant copies of this work

---

163. See note 160 above.
164. Wilmart, *op. cit.*
165. *Philokalia* 1, 38–43.
166. ES, 31.
167. A. and C. Guillaumont, *op. cit.,* 173–5.
168. *Loc. cit.*
169. This is printed in PG 79:1093–1140, among the works of St Nilus.

ascribe it to Evagrius. There are also three distinct Syriac translations of this work.[170]

10. *Treatise on Various Evil Thoughts* (*Capita Cognoscitiva* is the title used by one editor)[171]

This is preserved in Greek, and has also appeared in the *Philokalia* under the name of Evagrius. There are two distinct Greek recensions of this work, and Muyldermans has studied the Syriac tradition.[172] There is some hesitation in the Greek tradition about ascribing this to Evagrius, but the evidence is heavily in favor of ascribing it to him.

11. *Protrepticus* and *Paraeneticus*

These two works were addressed to a monk and deal with such questions as prayer, psalmody and other topics of monastic interest. Although it has been called into question by one scholar, the Evagrian authorship seems quite certain.[173] They have been edited at the head of the collection of letters in Frankenberg's edition. They are preserved only in the Syriac translation, not in the original Greek.[174]

12. *Letters*

The sixty-two letters preserved in Syriac are an important part of his work. For one thing they form probably the most ancient and complete collection of the entire Syriac literature.[175] For under-

---

170. ES, 46f.

171. PG 79:1200–1233, among the works of St Nilus. It is also included in the *Philokalia,* 1, 44–57.

172. Actually Muyldermans decides that this work is factitious, being made up by some later editor of collections of sentences from other works of Evagrius. ES, 79–80.

173. *Ibid.,* 75.

174. Possibly too in the Armenian under the title *Sermo exhortationis,* Frankenberg, pp. 124–280. Cf. I. Hausherr, "Les versions syriaque et arménienne d'Evagre le Pontique," *Orientalia Christiana,* 22 (1931), 74.

175. ES, 76.

standing the thought of Evagrius his letters are quite essential. In particular the letter to Melania, which is listed separately from the collection of sixty-two letters just mentioned. It explains a number of important Evagrian concepts, not all of which are orthodox.[176] The letters are addressed to Melania for the most part,[177] but others to whom letters are addressed are St Basil and St Gregory of Nazianzen.[178] A number of these letters are preserved also in Armenian and the important Letter Eight of St Basil, as it has been called, is still preserved in Greek having been transmitted among the letters of Basil.[179]

13. *Scriptural Commentaries*

Although Socrates and Gennadius and Palladius have all referred to certain of Evagrius' works by name, none of the ancients has stated that he also wrote commentaries on Scripture. Yet the fact is now certain. The most important of these commentaries is the *Commentary on the Psalms* which was preserved among the works of Origen, being ascribed to the latter. In 1939 von Balthasar studied the text and on the basis of its contents concluded that it was a work of Evagrius.[180] In 1960, Rondeau discovered in the Vatican library the manuscript evidence for Evagrian authorship of this work.[181] Actually this commentary is a series of sentences which represent highly personal reflections upon the text of the Psalms rather than a commentary in the usual sense of that word. It is quite important for a fuller understanding of Evagrian Christology.

Other commentaries on the Scriptures which are extant only in fragments deal with the books of Job and Proverbs. There are also the *De Seraphim*[182] dealing with the vision of Isaiah and *De Cherubim*

---

176. *Ibid.*, 78.   177. *Ibid.*, 77.   178. *Ibid.*, 78.

179. See the work by R. Melcher, *op. cit.* It has been edited recently in a critical edition: *Saint Basile, Lettres,* ed. Y. Courtonne, vol. 1 (Paris, 1957), 22–37.

180. H. U. von Balthasar, "Die Hiera des Evagrius Pontikus," *Zeitschrift für katholische Theologie,* 63 (1939), 86ff. and 181ff.

181. M. J. Rondeau, *op. cit.*

182. J. Muyldermans, "Sur les Séraphins et sur les Cherubins d'Evagre le Pontique dans les versions syriaque et arménienne," *Muséon,* 59 (1946), 367–79.

commenting on the vision of Ezechiel.[183] Finally a commentary on the *Pater noster* is known to have been written by him.

14. *Various Ascetic Treatises*

Muyldermans has published a group of Evagrian texts dealing with ascetic topics such as fasting, silence, humility, the signs of the state of quiet, the just man and the perfect man and still others.[184] All of these are preserved in the Syriac and prior to this edition were pretty much forgotten. Some of them are of considerable interest especially the short treatise entitled *De Justis et Perfectis*.[185] There are some sixteen such short treatises edited by Muyldermans.

Works of Doubtful Authenticity

1. *De Malignis Cogitationibus*

This work is quite likely from the pen of Evagrius[186]. It is extant in both Syriac and Greek.[187] The Syriac version however is a good deal shorter than the Greek text printed by Migne.

2. *Collections of Sentences*

A number of collections of sentences are extant under the names of Evagrius and Nilus in the tradition. The precise author has not yet been adequately established even though one of these collections, an alphabetical series, is found among the works of Evagrius in the Migne edition[188] and three others are found among the works of

---

183. *Ibid.*

184. ES, 105ff. Muyldermans also makes the interesting observation that in the Syriac literature there are a large number of mss. which contain collections of excerpts from various works of Evagrius. These collections were made for the use of monks in their *lectio divina,* and they constitute clear evidence for the wide popularity of Evagrius among the monks of various periods.

185. ES, 81f.   186. ES, 38.

187. It is printed in the Greek version in PG 79:1199–1234.

188. In PG 40:1268–69.

Nilus.[189] This type of literature has been influenced by the Greek gnomic style[190] but also by the biblical collections of aphorisms, especially *Proverbs*.

EVAGRIUS THE WRITER

Evagrius was a born writer. It is evident from his early activities in Constantinople that he had a gift of eloquence which soon put him in the public eye. He became known as an important speaker and was an excellent debater.[191] He did not altogether give up this activity even in his later years in the desert, but engaged in teaching and on occasional visits to Alexandria successfully preached against heresy.[192]

However, his style as a writer betrays very little of the sort of eloquence which was admired in the Greek world of his day. Evagrius carried his asceticism even into his writing and exercised a severe restraint which rarely gave free rein to his pen. The monk is always in evidence with insistence on a gravity and concentration of expression which would become oppressive were it not for the clear light of insight and the occasional flash of brilliance which lightens the whole. His aim was a conciseness of expression, and he achieved this purpose through the perfecting of his use of the "sentence," or gnomic saying. But he occasionally makes use of more descriptive, detailed style, as in the analysis of the various passions. In this case his native power of observation and accuracy of detail as well as the choice of precisely the telling gesture are striking and mark him out as the writer of genius. One of the best instances of this more descriptive style is found in the chapter of the *Praktikos* dealing with the vice of *acedia*.[193]

---

189. In PG 79:1236–64.

190. Bardenhewer refers to Evagrius as the "first Christian writer of gnomic literature" (*op. cit.,* 97). Cf. also A. and C. Guillamont, "Traité pratique," SC 170, 113f. for a thorough discussion of Evagrius' use of that form.

191. LH, 38:2, p. 111. 192. Festugière, *op. cit.,* 123.

193. C. 12 of the section: "The eight kinds of evil thoughts."

In fact it was in the area of descriptive psychology that Evagrius exercised one of his chief influences on later monastic tradition. He found in the desert tradition already a considerable body of teaching concerning the various passions and *logismoi* (passionate thoughts) which was the fruit of a practical experience of many years on the part of the more experienced monks. But he was the first to classify them into an ordered series of eight types of passionate thoughts.[194] He gave considerable place to these *logismoi* in his ascetic system. So he occupied himself with making the most accurate observations and descriptions of their dynamisms and operations. He was careful to describe the patterns of activity which characterized them and to indicate their inter-relations among themselves.[195] His work in this area became the classic and when John Cassian wished to teach the western monks the desert doctrine on the *logismoi* he could find no better source than the writings of Evagrius.[196]

The fact that Evagrius gave such prominence to psychology of a practical, experiential kind is another indication that he was influenced more by the desert tradition and by the lived experience of the spiritual life than is recognized by those scholars who see in him only the systematizer and the systematic philosopher. Indeed it was precisely this elemental concern with human experience as well as with the more theological aspects of the spiritual life that did so much to make his writings popular even among the monks

194. I. Hausherr, "L'origine de la théorie orientale des huit péchés capitaux." *Orientalia Christiana,* 30 (1933), 173.

195. The conviction that the dynamic relations among the passions was one of the most useful and significant things about their operations that the monk could understand is one of the most remarkable features of Evagrius' study of the *logismoi.* It puts him in the line of great practical-descriptive psychologists and relates him, in this respect, to the work of Freud.

196. See for instance Cassian's description of *acedia* as found in his *Institutes,* 10, 1, 2. It is not without significance that Cassian devotes so much space to this problem to which Evagrius himself gave so much stress. See SC 109, 384ff. Hausherr has pointed out that for Evagrius *apatheia* implies passive purification (See *OCP,* 12 [1946], 5–46). A full study of *acedia* has been done recently: S. Wenzel, *The Sin of Sloth: Acedia in Medieval Thought and Literature* (Chapel Hill, 1967).

who were often not intellectual in their approach to the spiritual life. In this he stands far removed from a writer like Pseudo-Denis, for instance, whose framework for his spiritual teaching is a Neoplatonic cosmology. Where Evagrius also elaborated a highly systematic philosophical cosmology, he was far less successful as a writer and theologian. He was a much better analyst of the human psyche than a theoretical thinker as regards his orthodoxy.

Another aspect of Evagrius' writing which is worth noting is the form he chooses to present his thought. The two works translated in this volume are both written in the form of sentences. There is nothing original in this form, for it was used by writers in the Greek world for a long time before Evagrius. The gnomic sayings, and especially important for Evagrius, the *Sentences* of Sextus made use of this literary genre. But Evagrius did make an original structure from this form. The highly polished, concise sentences which he composed were collected into groups, often of a hundred, and edited under the name of Century. This is actually quite an artificial process. Nowhere perhaps is that more evident than in the work on prayer which is translated in this volume. It contains 153 sentences or chapters so as to correspond with the number of fish caught by the disciples in the miraculous catch (Jn 21:11).

But in fact the Century form became quite popular. And, since it was Evagrius who first conceived of this approach to editing collections of sayings,[197] he stands as the initiator of a literary form which has a pedagogy all its own and is well adapted for meditation.

197. For a discussion of the Century in Byzantine literature see I. Hausherr, DS 2:416ff. (1938): "Centuries." Some interesting observations on the sentence form as a literary genre are to be found in F. Schlegel who wrote his philosophical teaching in the form of *Fragments* for the same kind of reason, so it seems to us, that Evagrius used the sentences: to express the incompleteness of human thought and its mysteriousness. See H. J. Forstman, "The Understanding of Language by Friedrich Schlegel and Schleiermacher," *Soundings*, 51 (1968), 152. And in recent times one of the philosophers of modern culture has shown how the sentence form is still a type of literature that fits in with the TV age for it has the same kind of tendency to produce active participation on the part of the reader who is stimulated to complete the thought it utters and so to enter into it in depth. See M. McLuhan, *Understanding Media: the Extensions of Man* (New York, 1966), 30.

One of the reasons for its popularity as spiritual reading is that it allows one to begin and end wherever one wishes. In some sense the Century has no beginning and no end. Its construction is not based on the line of logical development but follows more complex psychological laws, and perhaps at times follows no law at all. This gives the over-all effect of approaching the same topic from different points of view or aspects, looking at it now from one side, now from another. It sets the truth before one as an object to encounter, to penetrate, to assimilate, rather than as an element of a complete logical analysis. Each separate sentence exists independently from one point of view, but at the same time it has a relationship with each of the ninety-nine other sentences which lend various shades of meaning to it.

All these factors went to make the Century a form much appreciated by the later Byzantine world. Some of its greatest spiritual masters saw in it the literary genre admirably suited to convey the mystery of a spiritual experience which was ever renewed in its concrete uniqueness and which always escaped the confining limits of logical analysis. Then too it had the additional advantage of providing short, concise sayings which the monks could readily memorize and ponder in their meditation or call to mind in times of trial. Authors like Diadoch of Photicus,[198] Maximus the Confessor,[199] and Symeon the New Theologian[200] were to continue the use of this genre begun by Evagrius and pass it on to a large number of other spiritual authors in the Byzantine world. Through the *Philokalia* it continues to be a widely read form of literature in the Greek and Russian Orthodox world.[201]

198. The sentences of Diadoch have been published in the collection of his works that appeared in SC, ed. E. des Places, 84, 163.

199. The Centuries of Maximus have been published in an English translation: *St Maximus the Confessor: the Ascetic Life, the Four Centuries on Charity*, trans. P. Sherwood, ACW 21 (1955).

200. Symeon's Centuries are found in: *Symeon Le Nouveau Théologien: Chapitres Théologiques, Gnostiques et Pratiques*, ed. A. Darrouzès, SC 51 (1957).

201. The Century is one of the more widely used literary forms in these collections of spiritual writings. Whether literally one hundred sentences are adhered to or not, the basic conception remains that of the Century. This is clear, for instance, for the case where Evagrius named his major work the

A last feature of Evagrius' style that bears mentioning is his marked preference for definitions. His works reveal a decided concern for precise and logical definition which is in contrast with his overall lack of concern to present the final work as an articulated logical whole. Evagrius' emphasis on conciseness and precision of analysis led him largely to avoid allegory, and this is a feature which sets him off strongly from most other early theologians and writers, notably Origen and Gregory of Nyssa. This characteristic often makes Evagrius' writings easier to comprehend and was one of the reasons that he succeeded in popularizing the thought of these two Fathers to so large an extent. In taking their ideas into his own system and stating them in his clearer fashion he spread their ideas among wider audiences, and in part to a different type of audience than they were accustomed to find.[202]

After Evagrius the Byzantine ascetic and mystical vocabulary undergoes little change of direction. It progresses rather by enriching its vocabulary with later contributions from its many great theologians, but the basic stock was the Evagrian contribution in the form in which he cast the many elements he himself had taken from an earlier tradition formed from many currents.[203]

DOCTRINE

The Cosmology

Although much can be done by way of presenting the systematic teaching in Evagrius' world of thought, yet there is an important

---

Six Centuries, even though they contained only ninety, each Century missing ten sentences. The Century form was to have a future in the Latin world as well as in the Byzantine tradition, as one may observe, for example, in the hundred chapters of the *Diadema Monachorum* of Smaragdus, abbot of St Mihiel at Verdun, in the Carolingian period. See PL 102:593–690, and Jean Leclercq's comments in his *Témoins de la spiritualité occidentale* (Paris, 1965). More recently there is the work by Claudel: *Cent phrases.*

202. W. Jaeger, *Two Rediscovered Works of Ancient Christian Literature: Gregory of Nyssa and Macarius* (Leiden, 1954), 230.

203. See the evaluation by J. Meyendorf, *loc. cit.* He considers Evagrius the

fact to keep in mind from the beginning. Evagrius' history prepares us to accept the fact that he was a complex person. From the highest social and intellectual life of his times he passed to the most austere and simple form of life known to his age. It would be perhaps too much to hope that any man would be able to completely integrate two worlds of culture so far removed from one another as these, especially since anyone capable of passing through both cultures would be quite likely to be somewhat of a complex person to begin with. In any case it seems clear that, while Evagrius achieved an uncommon degree of integration and balance and gave the impression of a man fully at one with himself and his world at the end of his life,[204] he made no successful attempt to integrate into a single whole the various traditions by which he was formed.

Nor has any modern scholar so far been able to demonstrate the organic unity of Evagrius the Hellenistic thinker with the monk Evagrius, formed by Macarius and the other masters of the Coptic desert tradition.

St Basil first, then Gregory of Nazianzen, the great Theologian of the Trinity, and then Gregory of Nyssa, each exercised a direct intellectual and personal influence upon Evagrius while he was still quite young. And above all there is the giant of the early theologians, Origen, who strongly influenced all three of the Cappadocian Fathers and whose works Evagrius himself read. Clement of Alexandria too was influential. This is true especially with regard to the concept of *apatheia,* which Origen did not take up but which played a prominent part in Clement's asceticism and, under his influence, in Evagrius' thought also. The earlier *Eklogoi propheticae*

---

first great organizer of the monastic doctrine on prayer and the one who, in his *Chapters on Prayer,* gave a mystical vocabulary as well as a spiritual doctrine to subsequent generations of monks.

204. LH 38:13, p. 113.

205. The *Eklogoi propheticae* and the *Excerpta* are selections from works of ancient literature made by Clement of Alexandria which, as Bousset points out, give a singular emphasis to gnosis as an important activity of man. The same author considers that Evagrius' stress upon contemplation is so forceful

influenced Evagrius very deeply.[205] The list could be still further lengthened.[206]

There is the list of Egyptian antecedents to reckon with also. The list here is no less lengthy and no less eminent than the Greek one. It includes such personages as Macarius the Great, Macarius of Alexandria, Paphnutius,[207] Ammonius Parotes,[208] and, through his posthumous influence, the greatest of them, Blessed Anthony.[209]

Up to the present most of the scholars' attention has been given to that side of Evagrius' teaching which brought upon him the charge of heresy and the condemnation of the Church. Even those who recognize the basically Christian inspiration of his thought, such as Karl Rahner,[210] make no serious attempt to present it either as a system that stands alone or as an organic part of his thought as a whole. It is seen as a fact, but as a fact that resists analysis. This defect in our understanding of Evagrius is a serious one. Yet it is largely overlooked. The best of recent studies on his thought, that

---

as to align him with these works more than with Origen or Clement. Bousset, *op. cit.,* 3 "Evagriosstudien."

206. Such a list would include the Stoic philosophers and the Pythagorean Sextus (in the Armenian tradition the Sentences of Sextus are ascribed to Evagrius), whose morality was to impress itself upon the spirit of Evagrius. See H. Chadwick, *The Sentences of Sextus* (Cambridge, 1959), 162. Plotinus and other Neo-platonists too would find a prominent place in this list.

207. Paphnutius is particularly important for he is made to play a central role in the dialogues that Cassian records in his *Conferences.* His doctrine is very much reminiscent of that of Evagrius, and, indeed, we are informed by Palladius that Evagrius visited and spoke with this venerable father. LH 47:3, p. 125. For the teaching of Paphnutius, Cassian, *Conferences,* 3:1–22; PL 49:558–81.

208. Ammonius was already quite familiar with both Origen and with the desert tradition by the time Evagrius arrived in Nitria. It seems quite likely that he exerted considerable influence upon Evagrius at first.

209. In the LH 21:7, p. 73, St Anthony is referred to simply as "The Great One," and this is during the period of Evagrius' sojourn in Egypt. Indeed, some of the ideas which seem to be so characteristically Evagrian are to be found in the teaching of Anthony as presented by St Athanasius. Cf. *St Athanasius, The Life of St Anthony,* trans. R. Meyer, ACW 10 (1950), 50, where the concept of *apatheia* is suggested and related to the brightness of one's own soul.

210. K. Rahner, *op. cit.,* 22.

of Guillaumont,[211] except for a point here and there, notably his teaching on creation, does not deal with this difficulty. He makes an admirable study of the Evagrian cosmology and of his *Weltanschauung* as a whole, giving a very satisfying account of the Hellenistically inspired system, But what its relations are to his sacramentology, his view of the priesthood, his doctrine of the Church, all of which Evagrius deals with or at least mentions in the two works translated in this volume, is not studied.[212] Perhaps the best that can be done at this moment is simply to underline that, while we can present his thought as a developed theological and cosmological system, there yet remains the somewhat embarrassing fact that there are clear and strong assertions found in both the *Chapters on Prayer* and the *Praktikos,* as well as in others of his works and sayings, which do not fit into this system.[213] Their precise relation seems not to have been worked out by Evagrius himself. He may not have been aware of the contradictions. On the other hand, it is certainly not inconceivable that he chose to allow such discrepancies to remain. We may suppose that he was too much of a realist to attempt to enclose all of life in a rigid theoretic framework. In any case the fact is

211. We are thinking here of Guillaumont's *Les 'Kephalaia Gnostica.'*

212. For instance, Evagrius teaches that pure prayer takes place without images. At the same time he finds another, much more traditional way of describing the summit of the spiritual life: "If you can make deep thought about God have dominion in yourself, you can overcome all passions and you will be worthy of the perfection of the love of Christ." (Budge, *op. cit.,* 1017.) That Evagrius himself was well aware of the tension between these two traditions is well illustrated by a story recounting one of his conversations with one of the Fathers:

> On one occasion Abba Evagrius said to Abba Arsenius: "Since we are not without learning according to the world . . . (how is it that) the Egyptian villagers possess such excellences?" Abba Arsenius replied to him: "We possess nothing whatever from the learning of the world but these Egyptian villagers have acquired spiritual excellences through their labors." Budge, 882f.

213. T. Spidlik in a review of Guillaumont's study of Evagrius also arrived at the conclusion that Evagrius' doctrine is more traditional than Guillaumont believes it to be. He holds that his spiritual teaching, precisely because it is so traditional, is separable from his cosmological speculations, whereas Guillaumont holds the contrary. See *OCP,* 31 (1965), 422.

there: there remain tensions and conflicts, even in his carefully constructed works, which he did not attempt to resolve.[214]

The *Kephalaia Gnostica,* supplemented by the Epistle to Melania, are the chief sources for the analysis of his implicit world-view and theological system. They provide adequate materials to reconstruct the logically consistent and elaborate structure of the Hellenistically influenced segment of Evagrius' thought. The following description, which in large measure follows Guillaumont's study,[215] will give the main outlines of this system.

In the beginning there existed a single Henad, that is to say a single, undivided, integral whole whose nature was pure intelligence. It had been created by the Primitive Monad, or rather Henad. (Both these terms mean a simple unity; the second is the one Evagrius used. Origen had used the first.) Because of negligence these bodiless spirits after their multiplication fell away from their original state of mutual equality, where they had but a single activity and purpose: that of contemplating God (the Primitive Henad) in a simple eternal glance of essential knowledge.[216] This primitive state of unity with God is evidently a moral union only, not a metaphysical one in the fullest sense of the word, for it admits of being ruptured through moral fault. Nevertheless, it does have decidedly metaphysical consequences for it occasions the *second creation.* The fall itself is termed the *movement* (κίνησις). The decree which God enacts in response to this *movement* is called the *judgment* (κρῆσις). Thus the fall and its consequence is not a mere inevitable and necessary natural result of this carelessness, but it is rather the result of a free decree on the part of God. Consequently creatures are not mere degradated phases of a basically Divine Being, as the Neoplatonists taught. Evagrius does not hold to an emanational philosophy.[217]

214. Guillaumont, 336–37, mentions that he realizes too the complexity of Evagrian thought and that Origenism is but a part of it. He promises a more careful and thorough study of the question of the organic unity of this thought in a future publication.

215. Guillaumont, 37ff.

216. *Ibid.*

217. Guillaumont, 42, note 76.

The result of this *judgment* is the *second creation*. This is the origin of the cosmos, the organized world of bodies, the visible creation. It is ruled over by the God who is its Creator, and under this aspect, as ruler and protector, he is known as *Providence*.[218] Creation for Evagrius has a positive value, and nature is, in itself, good.

The fate of the individual spirits depends upon the degree of their guilt. They pass into bodies which are more or less material, more or less dark, more or less thick.

The angels form part of this material cosmos for they too have bodies. But their bodies are made of fire.[219] Thus they are very light, subtle and relatively unconfined by the thickness of matter. Other intelligences pass through this angelic stage to a lower one. They enter the world of visible bodies, in contrast to the invisible angelic bodies. Their bodies are thickened, above all by passion, by sensuality and by anger.[220] Those which are moderately dominated by such passion, above all by sensuality, are human beings. Human bodies occupy an intermediate position in the scale of fallen intelligences. Their bodies are formed from earth.

The demons occupy the last rung on the ladder. Their bodies are the darkest, most immersed in matter, most thickened by hatred, anger and resentment, most devoid of light. They consist of air, which being devoid of light, is ice-cold.[221]

Thus the position occupied in this ontological scale of beings is determined by the measure of ignorance of God. This, in turn, is proportioned to guilt.[222]

---

218. This emphasis on Providence is not the only element of Stoic thought which has found its way into Evagrian theology (see Guillaumont, 37–38). But whether this came directly from the Stoics or from Didymus the Blind is an open question. We know that Evagrius took the teaching of Didymus very much to heart with regard to this point: he relates it to Didymus in *Gnostikos*, 150, as Viller, *op. cit.*, 244, points out.

219. *Six Centuries*, 1:11. (Hereafter references to this work will be given imply according to the number, e.g. 1:68).

220. Thus the ascetic life, through purifying the soul of the passions, leads to putting on the new spiritual body even here on earth. See 1:11.

221. 6:25.

222. See for instance 1:68.

Not only do bodies arise from this creation, but souls also result from it. They too are part of the fall. Indeed, the same intelligence which was once a pure intelligence, without becoming another person, or more exactly another being, becomes a soul (ψυχή).

Now one of the outstanding characteristics of a soul, or psyche, is affectivity. The psyche is the seat of the passions. It is involved in varying measure with the body of the fallen intelligence (νοῦς). In the angels it is the intelligence that predominates; in man and in the demons, the psyche with its complex of passions. In man it is the passions associated with sensuality (ἐπιθυμία) that predominate; in the demons, those arising from irascibility (θύμος). This then is the make-up of the second creation, the schema which locates the position of the rational creatures after their *movement*.

In their original state these intelligent creatures were known as the *first creatures*, but in the process of being formed into beings with corporality as a part of their condition, they become *second creatures*. Along with the creation of bodies there takes place the creation of the particular world which is suited to them. The angelic creatures with their bodies of fire move in their own proper ambient. The same thing holds true for man and the demons. The environment is suited to the merit and to the qualities of each.

Although the second creation is the result of a fall and a decree of punishment on the part of God, yet at the same time Evagrius considers it an act of mercy. Were it not for the material world and the corporal substance joined to the rational nature (λόγικος), this creature would be in a position where it could not achieve liberation from its guilt, and so would remain in ignorance about God. Indeed, it is this ignorance of God that constitutes the great evil for the *second creatures* of all degrees. It is healed through the activity proper to rational nature's contemplation. Having lost their primitive intuitional knowledge of God they are yet provided with the type and measure of knowledge of him which is suited to their position in the cosmic ladder. Evil men, for instance, possess only a very rudimentary form of contemplation (παχεία) which gives little penetration into the true meaning of things.

Angelic knowledge, on the other hand, is known as the *first natural contemplation.*[223] Those men who, by the practice of prayer and asceticism become worthy of it, possess *second natural contemplation.* Above both these forms there remains a primeval form known as *essential contemplation* (θεωρία οὐσιώδης) which is the activity of only those creatures who are totally purified of all passion of a disordered sort and of all images which could interfere with such an exalted form of understanding.

Wherever one finds himself situated on this scale of life he has the duty of advancing higher through the various intermediate stages until he returns to the primitive state. Man, therefore, must advance by means of purification so that he attains by ascesis and prayer to the angelic state with its more spiritual form of knowledge. As the individual advances from one type of knowledge to another he puts on the form of body, or rather is transformed into that bodily form, which is appropriate to his new state, and at the same time enters the environmental conditions appropriate to that body.

One of the conclusions to be drawn from this analysis of Evagrian teaching is that basically it is not the nature of the rational creature that establishes him in his individual ontological position, but rather his contemplation. Fundamentally, all rational beings are the same; they are intelligences (νόες).

This process leads to the union with God that they obtained formerly, prior to the second creation, and to the primeval knowledge. It is the task of creatures to move steadily upwards to this union with God, though it can also happen that, through negligences repeated, they move down the scale, further away from him. This process of ascent takes place under the benevolent influence of God's grace and through the good services of exceptionally pure spirits. Angels who are very pure and most favorable to man's salvation may even assume a lower position on the world scale so

223. The problem of translating the Greek word θεωρία, which we have called "contemplation," is an old one. For a discussion of the problems it represents see I. Hausherr, "Les versions syriaque et arménienne d'Evagre le Pontique," *Orientalia Christiana,* 22 (1931), 75 and esp. the interesting footnote 1 citing F. S. Marsh on this problem. The latter feels that at times it is better translated as "mystery," "secret," etc. rather than "contemplation."

as to be able to enlighten and otherwise assist men on their upward path. Christ himself is precisely such an intelligence.

Christology

There was one single intelligence who did not fall into negligence, but who remained faithful to the contemplation and possession of the *essential knowledge*. This means that he alone remained united to God. This intelligence was possessed, as a result, unceasingly by the Word of God. Through the union with the Word this intelligence is God.

The whole second creation is the work of this Savior, who is Christ. The multifaceted wisdom with which the second creation is achieved fills all things and provides the rational creatures with their proper object for *theoria physike*, the contemplation of nature which leads to an increase of the knowledge of God. This same Christ is the judge who decrees all the judgments consequent upon every new *movement*. The Incarnation was another step in this work of salvation. It is an indication of the benevolence of this all-pure Christ that he willingly lowered himself to help man.

This, however, is but one phase of redemption. There is still another, *the seventh day*, which is an eschatological period characterized by the rule of Christ over all rational creatures. The demons too fall under his rule, for they also are to pass through successive stages and attain, increasingly, purity of heart. When all creatures have attained to the stage of angelic purity and its proper contemplation and its spiritual body of fire, then the first eschatological period is established. This period in turn shall give way to a second, known as *the eighth day*. This eighth day will mark the end of the reign of Christ when all the intelligences return to the primitive unity with God, and all rational creatures become ἰσοχρίστοι, fully equal to Christ. All the second creation will be abolished, and this includes bodies in all their forms. Indeed, matter itself will be done away with, and all the implications of matter such as diversity, multiplicity and number. The original integral Henad is reconstituted. The great cosmic round-dance has come to an end. All things have returned to union with their beginning, until union itself gives way to unity.[224]

This is the cosmology of Evagrius and his salvation history as it appears in his most theoretical works, notably the *Kephalaia Gnostica* as seen through the perspectives of the important first part of the *Letter to Melania*.[225] We cannot comment on the various parts of it in a work of limited dimensions, but its defects are obvious. One could even wonder what has become of biblical Christianity in the system of Evagrius, were this all that we had to go on in evaluating the Evagrian spirituality. Fortunately, it is not all. We have his more empirical works, above all the two works translated in this volume.

Before analyzing their contents to discern the structure of his ascetic system it may be well to remark that these other works are oriented much more toward experience than speculation. They give no clear indications of these highly philosophical speculations. This is so true that, until the recovery of the original version of the *Kephalaia Gnostica* some fifteen years ago, it was not at all evident that Evagrius was justly judged to be a teacher of those dogmas for which the Council in 553 had condemned him. Some of the most judicious of theologians and Church historians, in fact, had absolved

---

224. A striking feature of this *Weltanschauung* is the many features it shares with certain theologies found in the Judeo-Christian tradition. The large place given to demons and angels; the ascent of souls through the various heavens (cf. *The Ascension of Isaias*); the marked eschatological bias which is a feature of this tradition, and which gives the lie to the assertion made by some (e.g. F. M. Cross, *The Ancient Library of Qumran* [New York, 1958], 74) that under contact with Hellenistic thought Christianity lost its eschatological tension. Evagrius is a prime instance where such is not the case, and the whole history of monasticism bears witness to the preservation of an element of the eschatological within the Church. Monasticism understands itself precisely as eschatologically oriented. For the pertinent data on the Judeo-Christian tradition see the important work by J. Daniélou, *The Theology of Jewish Christianity* (London, 1964), esp. 358f.

225. Frankenberg, *op. cit.*, 612–619. The second part of this letter, which gives a great deal of attention to the mysteries of Christ, has been discovered and published more recently by G. Vitestam. See note 31 of the Introduction to the *Praktikos,* below, p. 10.

Evagrius of these charges.[226] They had based their judgment on the Evagrius of the *Praktikos* and *Antirrheticus* and of the *Apophthegmata;* and had they known that the *Chapters on Prayer* was his, they would have felt only more secure in this judgment, as Hausherr points out.[227]

With our present knowledge of his authorship of the *Kephalaia Gnostica* and the first part of *Epistle to Melania,* however, there remains no doubt that the charges brought against him are correct[228] though they were made with undue harshness and without the restraint which was due to his personal sanctity and good faith.

Ascetic and Mystical Theology

Evagrius was the first important writer among the monks of the desert. He was further the first to organize into a coherent system the teachings of the Desert Fathers on prayer.[229] To be sure, this part of Evagrius' system is of a piece with the desert tradition that had been developed over several generations prior to his arrival in Egypt. The young monk recently arrived from Jerusalem, from the agony of his painful conversion and his backsliding and re-conversion, had accepted the monastic life with all his heart. He would come as a disciple. And he would learn his lesson well from the Fathers, especially from both of the famous Macarii. More, he would give a new form and an enhanced force of expression to this tradition which, after his work, would ever bear the mark of his influence.

Evagrius defined for the monks in his circle his own concept of the ascetic life. It is "the spiritual method whose aim it is to purify the part of the soul that is the seat of the passions."[230] The defini-

226. Tillemont, Duschesne and Butler to name but three. Guillaumont remarks on this, p. 40, notes 69f.

227. I. Hausherr, "Le traité d'oraison d'Evagre le Pontique," RAM, 15 (1934), 39f.

228. Guillaumont, 256f.

229. J. Meyendorf, *op. cit.,* 19.   230. *Praktikos,* 50.

F

tion is programatic: Evagrius is going to set forth the method for attaining purity of heart through the sublimation and right ordering of the emotions, or as he would call them, the passions.

Evagrius was to become the anatomist of the passions of the psyche both in their manifestations in behavior and in their intra-psychic activity. He had an extremely dynamic view of their operations. And this quite naturally extended to their good and wholesome operations as well as to their disordered tendencies. Here is the speech that he recommends for the novice to hear upon receiving the monastic habit. It gives some idea of his manner of clarifying and uniting into a single whole the operations of the emotions: "The fear of God strengthens faith, my son, and con-tinence in turn strengthens this fear. Patience and hope make this latter virtue solid beyond all shaking and they also give birth to *apatheia*. Now this *apatheia* has a child called *agape* who keeps the door to deep knowledge of the created universe. Finally, to this knowledge succeed theology[231] and the supreme beatitude."[232]

This passage is noteworthy from another point of view, for it locates in a specifically Christian and biblical context the key-stone of his whole structure of ascetic practice, *apatheia*.[233] Thus *apatheia*,

231. For Evagrius' definition of theology, *Praktikos*, 60. It amounts to the experiential knowledge of God through the highest form of prayer.

232. *Letter to Anatolius*, below, p. 14.

233. The recently discovered Coptic *Gospel of Thomas* lends support to the view that *apatheia* as a concept is rooted rather in the biblical than in the Greek world, as it is used by the Fathers of the Church. Not only does one *logia* (n. 22) refer to the interior simplicity that is implied by *apatheia* in the patristic tradition, but two of the *logia* use the Coptic term for monk as the term describing the one who has attained to this simplicity. This fact is all the more significant in that the work is deeply rooted in the Bible and probably pre-serves some of the original sayings of Jesus. It is therefore not unlikely that this theme formed an element of the primitive catechesis and derived from the teaching of our Lord himself. See M. Harl, "A propos des logia de Jésus: le sens du mot μόναχος," *Revue des études grecques*, 63 (Paris, 1960), 464–474, as reported and discussed in A. Louf, *et. al.*, *The Message of Monastic Spirituality*, trans. L. Stevens (New York, 1964), 41f. G. Quispel has also studied this term in the same text, and observes that it replaces the word for "virgins" of the original gospel parable. It thus appears to be a technical term. There is a corresponding term in the Hebrew text of the "Rule for the Community"

far from being a mere transposition of the Stoic experience, is rather akin to the fear of the Lord. Still more significantly, it is parent to love, to *agape*. Because *apatheia* is the immediate aim of ascetic practice for Evagrius and because in the treatises translated in this volume it occupies so important a position, we would do well to examine his understanding of it quite carefully.

The word itself is indeed taken from the Stoic philosophers, where it had a long and venerable history. In fact even before the Stoics it had a development centuries long in the Greek philosophical tradition.[234] It was taken over by the Christians early, long before Evagrius. Indeed, it was used by the most orthodox of Fathers and was applied to Christ himself. St Ignatius of Antioch is the first to employ it in this way.[235] Other orthodox Fathers adopted it as well. St Anthanasius made considerable use of it in his arguments against the Arians, likewise applying it to the man-God, Jesus.[236] But it was Clement of Alexandria who took it over into his ascetical theology. He made it, in fact, a cornerstone of his spiritual edifice. He is somewhat idealistic in the description he gives of the peace possessed by the man who attains to this state. Yet he does not go so far as to convey that all emotion is extinguished in the man who possesses this state of harmony. Rather he sees it as the full possession, under the influence of divine contemplation, of the affective faculties, so that disordered passions are resolved into a state of abiding calm. It seems to us that Clement exaggerates man's achievement in this area when he speaks of his attaining a state even here on earth where he is not exposed to desire and lacks nothing of spiritual

---

from Qumran, *janid*, which designates a "celibate" member of the community. See *Cistercian Studies*, 3 (1968), (97). Does this mean that the concept "monk" derives from Judaism?

234. For a thorough discussion of the Greek tradition of *apatheia*, T. Ruther, *Die Sittliche Forderung der Apatheia* (Freiburg, 1949), 3–19. A. and C. Guillaumont, TP, 93f. also study *apatheia* in Evagrius.

235. *The Epistles of St Clement of Rome and St Ignatius of Antioch*, trans. J. Kleist, ACW 1 (1946), 63.

236. *St Athanasius: Discourses against the Arians*, trans. and ed. by J. H. Newman (Oxford, 1877), 449. For further references, *Lexicon Athanasianum*, Guido Müller (Berlin, 1952): "ἀπάθεια" and "ἀπάθης," 107–108.

goods.[237] On the other hand, mystics of more recent times than his have spoken the same language, St John of the Cross for one. Then too, St Theresa of Avila seems to have been very close to this state at the very end of her life, though she was less absolute in her expression of it than John of the Cross.

Origen himself was more cautious, for once, in his choice of terms. He seems to have avoided the word *apatheia* quite deliberately.[238] Because of the fact that Origen emphasizes so much the continual progress in the spiritual life, he is less inclined to speak of so perfect a state as *apatheia*. When he does, he gives it much less central a place in his system.[239] The term occurs often in the writings of the Cappadocians, but it is far less important for them than it is for either Evagrius or Clement.[240]

Evagrius, consequently, is going back beyond his immediate teachers, the Cappadocian Fathers, even back beyond Origen to Clement of Alexandria when he gives to this concept such prominence. It may well be that the desert tradition had influenced him in this, for the ideal of *apatheia* is prominently painted for us in the *Vita Antonii* by St Athanasius. St Anthony was to be the model for monks in this as in all other matters pertaining to the ascetic life.[241]

But Evagrius was to put his own stamp on this concept as well as on so many others. For him *apatheia* is more recognizably human than it is in Clement. Although it does represent a certain definitive state of arrival at a level of perfection, it represents only a relatively permanent state of deep calm, arising from the full and harmonious integration of the emotional life, under the influence of love. For him *apatheia* and *agape*, divine love, are but two aspects of a single reality. In fact, the offspring of *apatheia* is *agape*.[242] This is its first

---

237. L. Lorié, *Spiritual Terminology in the Latin Translations of the Vita Antonii* (Nijmegen, 1955), 123-24, where he discusses the *Stromata*, VI, 9, 71-72.

238. Bouyer, *op. cit.*, 298.   239. *Ibid.*, 297f.

240. *Patristic Greek Lexicon*, ed. W. H. Lampe (Oxford, 1961-68): "ἀπάθεια."

241. ACW 10:77. On the question of the biblical basis of *apatheia*, O. Rousseau, "Le rôle important du monachisme dans l'Eglise d'Orient," *Il Monachismo Orientale*, Orientalia Christiana Analecta, 153 (Rome, 1958), 40-41.

242. *Praktikos*, 81.

fruit and flower, so that where the first is found the second is present
also. The one supports and vitalizes the other, enabling its con-
tinuance and full expression. They are, as it were, the positive and
negative poles of a single field of force.[243]

What is the genealogy of this state of deep calm? According to
our author it is obtained through obedience to the commandments
of God and the practice of virtue.[244] It is worth noting that Evagrius
has an unusually strong confidence in the powers of such obedience
to achieve purity of heart in the monk. In this he is doubtless deeply
under the influence of St Basil, whose teaching gave such prominence to the commandments and to obedience in all its forms. This
confidence in obedience as a path to perfection is much stronger in
Evagrius than in many other mystical writers, notably Denis the
Areopagite.[245]

Conceived by obedience *apatheia* is preserved by fear of the
Lord.[246] It is nourished and grows through the practice of humility
and the cultivation of sorrow for sin.[247] Further, it never fully
stabilizes; it always requires a willingness to guard and protect it,
for it remains exposed to the assaults of the demons.[248] It has limits
that come from the human situation. For instance, it is too much to
expect that one should love all men with an equal love.[249] *Apatheia*
is not a leveling out of the human emotions to an equal degree of
indifference towards all men. No, it is a state where all men can be
loved, at least to the extent that one lives peacefully and without
resentment towards others.[250] Even so some will be loved more,
some less; Evagrius considers that this is no defect in the perfection

243. G. M. Columbás, "El concepto de Monje y Vida Monástica hasta
fines del Siglo V," *Studia Monastica*, 1 (1959), 298. He is following Hausherr
here.

244. *Praktikos*, 81.

245. I. Hausherr, "Les grands Courants de la Spiritualité Orientale," *OCP*,
1 (1935), 124.

246. *Praktikos*, 81.   247. 5:5.

248. *Praktikos*, 77 and 60. See Viller, *op. cit.*, 178.

249. *Ibid.*, 100.   250. *Ibid.*

of the state of *apatheia*. Lastly, this state admits of degrees and allows for a continuing growth.[251]

Still more basic—and this point has been contested by some—is the place occupied by grace in the acquisition of this state of soul. It is essential.[252] So is the ministration of the priest and the reception of the sacraments essential for the perfect purification of soul that is *apatheia*.[253] Indeed, it is the fruit of prayer, of the grace of the Holy Spirit, and the "power of Jesus Christ who makes me grow."[254] The content of the Evagrian *apatheia* is fully Christian beyond all cavil, both in its inspiration and in its aim. It is the art of achieving the right order of charity, as the medieval monks would speak of it,[255] that Evagrius describes when he writes on attaining to *apatheia*. In fact he states that *apatheia* makes one "worthy of the perfection of the love of Christ."[256]

There are a number of characteristics that indicate the presence of *apatheia* for Evagrius. Not the least interesting of these is what he has to say about its relation to dreams. For he understood the dynamic influence exercised upon the dream activity of man by the passions and emotions that filled his soul in the waking state too well to overlook the fact that purity of heart would be reflected in one's dreams. He asserts that one of the indications that a man has attained to *apatheia* is the absence of passion and disordered emotion from his dream images.[257] He goes on to state elsewhere[258] that under the influence of *apatheia* not only does a man remain free from passion when subject to the situations and events that tend to stimulate passion, but also—and he clearly considers this a greater achieve-

---

251. *Ibid.*, 60, where two types of *apatheia* are mentioned, perfect and imperfect, which implies the possibility of growth.

252. *Ibid.*, 100.   253. *Ibid.*   254. *Ibid.*

255. For instance *St Bernard de Clairvaux: Sermones super Cantica Canticorum*, ed. by J. Leclercq, C. Talbot and H. Rochais, Sermons 49 and 50 (Rome, 1958), 73ff.; trans. K. Walsh, *On the Song of Songs*, Cistercian Fathers Series 31. The theme of *ordinavit in me charitatem* is one of St Bernard's favorites and sums up for him the whole work of the spiritual life.

256. Budge, *op. cit.*, 1017.   257. *Praktikos*, 64.   258. *Ibid.*, 67, 34.

ment—when the very memory of such things is stirred, he nevertheless remains calm and at peace. Another sign of the presence of this state is the ability to pray without distraction.[259] Finally when the soul begins to see its own light, then it can be sure of having attained to the longed for goal of *apatheia*.[260]

Evagrius himself has grouped these various signs together for the convenience of the monk. He considered them so significant that he does not wish them to be either overlooked or forgotten too rapidly. Thus he collected his evidence in an impressive series of signs that would act as a forceful reminder to monks of the aim of their ascetic life, the purity of heart that he called *apatheia*, for to it is promised the Kingdom of Heaven that is the vision of God.[261]

Indeed, he tells us: "The Kingdom of Heaven is *apatheia* of the soul along with true knowledge of existing things."[262] Later on, when John Cassian would address himself to the western monks on the true aims of the ascetic life, he could find nothing better to put at the very head of his *Conferences* than this same *apatheia*,[263] though he was careful, of course, to employ a Latin equivalent that would not stir up the suspicions of the anti-Pelagians of his day. That equivalent was *puritas cordis*, purity of heart.[264]

The *apatheia* described by Evagrius differs from the *stabilitas* and *tranquilitas* of Jerome and some of the other Western Fathers in that these latter commonly refer to a state that is more or less transient.[265] *Apatheia*, on the other hand, for Evagrius is a permanent state and marks a decisive turning point in the spiritual itinerary of the Christian. It is the door to contemplation, or more exactly, its vestibule. For charity, the finest fruit of *apatheia*, is the door to contemplation.[266]

---

259. *Ibid.*, 69.

260. *Ibd.*, 64.

261. Mt 5:8.

262. *Praktikos*, 2.

263. J. Cassian, *Conferences*, 1:4; PL 49:486.

264. Lorié, *op. cit.*, 125–26, where it is pointed out that other equivalents of *apatheia* are *tranquilitas* and *stabilitas*.

265. Chadwick, *op. cit.* 84; also G. Bardy, DS 1:734 (1934): "*apatheia*."

266. *Letter to Anatolius*, below, p. 14.

Contemplation

For Evagrius *apatheia* is the health of the soul.[267] But alone it does not suffice for a complete return to health. "The effects of keeping the commandments (that is to say, *apatheia*) do not suffice to heal the powers of the soul completely. They must be complemented by a contemplative activity which is appropriate to these faculties and this activity must penetrate the spirit."[268] Contemplation in this view, then, is not a mere luxury for a few specially favored souls. It is the indispensable activity of every Christian who would become perfect.

Had Evagrius thought any differently, after all, he would hardly have been a Greek. And he certainly would not have been so fully a pupil of the great Alexandrians, especially of Clement. Was it not this Christian humanist who preserved to posterity the strongest expression of the place of contemplation in life that the Greek world has left us: θεωρία ἐστι τέλος τοῦ βίου, that is to say, the purpose of life is contemplation.[269] Hardly any spiritual writer before him had used the words for contemplation so frequently as he. Both θεωρία and γνῶσις occur abundantly in his vocabulary.[270]

Once *apatheia* with its attendant charity is achieved in a stable manner, contemplative activity, properly so called, becomes dominant. The first phase of the contemplative life he chose to call "contemplation of nature," θεωρία φυσική. Without trying to go into great detail on the precise nature of this stage of contemplation, we might point out that it includes penetration into the meaning of

267. *Praktikos,* 65. Possession of *apatheia* is clearly presumed here.

268. *Ibid.,* 79.

269. This saying of Anaxagoras of Clazomenes is preserved by Clement of Alexandria. *Clement d'Alexandrie: Les Stromates,* 2:21, vol. 2 trans. P. Camelot et Cl. Mondésert, SC 38 (Paris, 1954), 130. I. Hausherr, "Les grands courants de spiritualité orientale," *OCP,* 1 (1935), 121, has pointed out the relevance of this statement for understanding the Greek spirituality.

270. J. Le Maitre, R. Roques, M. Viller in DS 2:1776 (1950): "Contemplation," where it is pointed out that Clement uses these two terms more often than any other Greek author except Maximus the Confessor.

Scripture. Also included is the structured order of the universe, the varieties of natural phenomena and the natural symbols that fill our world—all these provide material for the pure of heart to grow in understanding of the ways of God with men, and so reveal something further about the nature of God himself.

But more significant than merely what it includes is the fact that it is more than a mere natural knowledge or poetic insight into the real connections of things, into their inner *logoi*. It is this, to be sure, but it has an added dimension to it. That is the moral dimension. For it is accessible only to the pure of heart.[271] In his commentary on the Psalms, Evagrius was to take up a definition that St Anthony had already employed, although he did not speak of the term *theoria physike*, when he spoke of the physical world as a book of God in which the Spirit can write.[272] From this contemplation one derives a knowledge of the attributes of God, rather than of his very nature. Thus it represents a real but intermediate stage of contemplation; in no wise does it imply unusual mystical graces. It is a more elemental knowledge than the contemplation of the Blessed Trinity. In holding the view that there are two degrees of contemplation he is in fundamental accord with the teaching of Gregory of Nyssa.[273]

Whereas in the inferior degree of contemplation, *theoria physike*, the monk does not attain to complete simplicity of thought, but remains in a state of multiplicity, the contrary is true in the higher contemplation, $\theta\epsilon\omega\rho\acute{\iota}\alpha$ $\tau\hat{\eta}s$ $\acute{\alpha}\gamma\acute{\iota}\alpha s$ $\tau\rho\acute{\iota}\alpha\delta os$.[274] The lower kind of contemplation further contrasts with the higher in that the former is attended by effort, struggle, and at times a degree of frustration.[275] The latter is marked by great peace and calm. It knows no frustration, but only the tranquility of possession.

---

271. 4:90.

272. The *Selecta in Psalmis* (PG 12:1661C—among the works of Origen). This passage is cited in the article by LeMaitre, Roques and Viller, DS 2:1777 (1952). Our discussion of contemplation owes a good deal to this highly informative article. Cf. also E. Jeauneau, *op. cit.*, 254, note 2, for this same theme in John Scotus and Maximus the Confessor; in addition, cf. *Praktikos*, below, ch. 92.

273. *Ibid.*, 1779. 274. *Chapters on Prayer*, 57. 275. DS 2:1778; also 1:65.

This higher form of contemplation has several names, such as the first contemplation (πρώτη θεωρία) or contemplation of the Blessed Trinity (θεωρία τῆς ἁγίας τρίαδος). It results in simple intuitive knowledge (γνῶσις μονοειδής) or again what he terms "essential knowledge" (γνῶσις οὐσιώδης). This last does not refer to a knowledge of the essence of God, a doctrine which Evagrius does not teach, but rather to an experimental knowledge of God. Nevertheless, though God can be known only as *present* and not in his essential nature, yet even this kind of penetration into the Divinity is an exalted state and as such is beyond the mere capacity of man. Man can only pray for it and humbly and gratefully receive it as a gift.[276] The other feature of this elevated contemplation is that it requires complete nudity of the intellect.[277] In this mysticism at its highest point it is the Blessed Trinity that is the object of vision. Only this vision is beyond form (μονοειδής; ψιλός); it is totally simple. No one has stressed this more forcefully than Evagrius did. The essential transcendence of God is a cornerstone of his mystical theology. It is this surpassing grandeur of the Divine Nature that demands such total purity, even nudity of the spirit of man, for like can be known only by like in his view. In adopting this position he is following the lead of the Platonic school,[278] but he speaks with a passion and insistence that bear witness to his own profound experience of the necessity of the utmost purification from all limiting concepts as well as from all moral impurity for the attainment of this knowledge of the Blessed Trinity.

Evagrius gives no precise description of the nature of this knowledge, but he does speak habitually of states of soul that accompany it. The most revealing ones are those which speak of the light phenomena that attend this contemplation. Already the Cappadocians had spoken in the same way; both Gregory of Nyssa[279] and St Basil had referred to the knowledge of God as being

276. 5:79.   277. 3:6, 21.

278. A. J. Festugière, *Contemplation et Vie Contemplative selon Platon* (Paris, 1950), 108.

279. *Gregorii Nysseni Opera Ascetica,* ed. W. Jaeger, J. Cavarnos, V. Callahan, "De institutione christiana" (Leiden, 1952), 48, 50.

heralded by the light shining in the soul. Indeed, Evagrius, in one passage, relies upon the witness and authority of Basil for teaching that pure prayer brings the soul to a glorious experience of interior light.[280] But his most renowned description of the light-mystique occurs in the following passage: "When the spirit has put off the old man to replace him with the new man, created by charity, then he will see that his own state at the time of prayer resembles that of a sapphire; it is as clear and bright as the very sky. The Scriptures refer to this experience as the place of God which was seen by our ancestors, the elders, at Mount Sinai."[281] In other words, the soul itself becomes the *locus visionis,* the place of vision, not of God as he is in himself, but as he makes his presence known. He shines in the soul as in a mirror.[282] The Septuagint[283] had introduced this expression of the "place of God" as a way of toning down the epiphany of Yahweh. To "see God" seemed too strong a saying.

The concept of the soul as the mirror of God is an important element in the anthropological doctrine of Evagrius, and it plays a central role in his mysticism as well. He tells us explicitly that "The image of God . . . is he who has become capable of the unity."[284] This unity, as we know, is Evagrius' way of saying that the soul has attained to the perfect knowledge of the Blessed Trinity in loving union. Indeed, the paraphrase adopted by the corrected Syriac version expresses it in these terms: "That man is the image of God who is capable of receiving the knowledge of the Blessed Trinity."[285] Consequently, for Evagrius, the very definition of man must be established in terms of his contemplation. It is contemplative union

280. Cf. DS 2:1781 with its references to *Gnostikos,* 147 and the *Supplement to Centuries,* 50.

281. PG 40:1244A. Though this is printed as a part of the *Praktikos* it is not in fact a part of this work.

282. This concept is already found in Gregory of Nyssa's *Commentary on the Canticle of Canticles* (PG 44:824C).

283. The Septuagint already makes the connection found in Evagrius between the place of God (ὁ τόπος τοῦ θεοῦ) and sapphire light: "They saw then the place where the God of Israel stood; and under his feet there was a kind of wrought-work as bright and clear as if made of sapphire." Ex 24:10-11.

284. 3:32.   285. *Ibid.*

with God which is man's ultimate end, and which establishes man in his full self-realization as the image of God. In this outlook man is not defined as a rational animal (Aristotle) but rather as a being created to be united with God in loving knowledge. This is, for our author, in the full sense of the word, a metaphysical statement, not only mystical and religious statement.[286] In the closing words of his treatise, *Gnostikos,* Evagrius has given us a characteristically lapidary phrase summarizing his view on this matter: "Hasten along to transform your image to the resemblance of the archetype . . . ."[287] This is the aim of life. In this work of transformation is summed up the meaning and purpose of human existence for Evagrius. It is all of man.

Prayer and Contemplation

Hausherr has shown that the deepest significance of the achievement of Evagrius' thought is situated precisely at the point where he identifies the highest form of contemplation with the state of pure prayer.[288] The man who truly prays is the man who has seen the place of God. This is what it means to be a theologian,[289] or as we should say today, a *mystic.* Not only do these two activities and states coincide at their highest states, they also coincide every step of the way.[290]

While Origen and Gregory of Nyssa had already taught the relationship that exists between prayer and the stages of the spiritual life, Evagrius goes beyond their position in the identification of the two, as two complementary aspects of a single whole. There is a

---

286. E. von Ivánka, *Plato Christianus* (Einsiedeln, 1964), 148; also Muyldermans, *op. cit.,* 164, for a citation from Evagrius' *Commentary on the Parables and Proverbs of Solomon,* 26.

287. *Gnostikos,* 151, cited in DS 2:1783 (1952): "Contemplation" by Le Maître, etc.

288. Hausherr, *Leçons,* 8ff.

289. *Chapters on Prayer,* 60.   290. Hausherr, 80–81.

profound psychology hidden beneath this doctrine; a psychology which realizes the dynamic connections between psychic images on the one hand and, on the other, the emotions and habitual attitudes both of mind and of affections. Only where mental and spiritual images are fully adapted to the pure light of God, so far as this can be, is it possible for man's attitudes and activities to achieve their full flowering in a harmony that resolves all earlier discords. These images are purified and transformed through contemplation of this same Divine Light as it shines in the mirror of the soul. Man cannot be perfected merely from action that proceeds from the exterior to the interior. He must be altered even in the depths of his spirit, where there lie hidden in the furthest recesses of his being unknown images, inaccessible to the external world save by some long-forgotten, distant paths which still exert their influence upon a man's attitudes and ways. Only when these images are healed and restored in the pristine light of a holy contemplation that reaches even thus far into the spirit of a man is the work of his salvation and of his perfection fully realized.

On the psychological plane, Evagrius' emphasis upon a contemplation so pure that it penetrates beyond all distinct, clearly defined (and so limited and limiting) images is wholly vindicated. Whether at the same time it meets all the demands of the Christian religion where the sacred humanity of Jesus is the focal point of all knowledge of God is quite another question. It is one that many, perhaps, would answer in the negative.

There can be little doubt that in his more theoretical works Evagrius does deviate too far from a life of prayer centered on the Incarnate Word of God. Yet, since he never had a chance to answer those who saw the implications of his teaching as a deviation from the orthodox faith, it is impossible to say precisely how he would have dealt with the objections that were raised against his Christology. In this he resembles, perhaps, Teilhard de Chardin.

We know that Evagrius had a great love of the sacraments and of the Eucharist in particular, for his last act was to receive Communion at the church on Epiphany, just prior to his death. He did not always give the central place to Christ in his teaching, however, even when perhaps he thought he was doing so. In this too he is a follower of Origen.[291] It is unfortunate that we have no commentary by Evagrius on that verse of St John which defines the essential nature of salvation for the Christian: "This is eternal life, that they may know you the only true God, and Jesus Christ whom you have sent."[292]

291. One of the clear indications of the complexity of Evagrian thought is his express statement that one must be always careful not to put Christ in the shade when read alongside the criticisms of those who find he has himself done precisely this. That Evagrius himself thought he had preserved orthodoxy is clear from his warning that we must be on guard lest while striving after mystical knowledge of God we should neglect the mystery of the Incarnation: ἵνα μή . . . τῇ θεωλογία προσέχοντες, τῆς οἰκονομίας καταφρονῶμεν (Cf. *Sancti Basilii Opera Omnia,* ed. Maurists (Paris, 1839) 3:116. But the problem of the place of the humanity of Christ in the higher stages of the spiritual life is in any case one that has long presented difficulties to mystics and theologians. Cassian had his difficulties with it too, as Chadwick indicates (Chadwick, *op. cit.,* 150) and even Teresa of Avila did not find it easy to deal with this problem.

292. Jn 17:3. For an interesting theological elaboration of this crucial point, see K. Rahner, "Die ewige Deutung der Menscheit Jesu für unser Gottes-verhältnis," *Schriften für Theologie* 3 (Einsiedeln, 1961), 47–60. More recently this problem comes up in the confrontation of Christian mysticism with Zen Buddhism. It is the major theme of an important study: William Johnston's "The Still Point" (New York, 1970).

PRAKTIKOS

INTRODUCTION

THE PRAKTIKOS is Evagrius' best known work on the ascetic life. In it he sets forth more completely than anywhere else his doctrine of ascesis. In writing it he had in mind primarily the needs of hermits, who, he tells us, are most frequently tempted by the demons by means of passionate thoughts.[1] But it has quite as much to say to Christians of all states as it does to solitaries, for they have no monopoly on the struggle against passionate thoughts.

This work is part of a larger book, though it was written as a whole that could be read independently. Evagrius himself[2] tells us of its relation to the *Gnostikos*[3] and the *Kephalaia Gnostica*.[4] While these last works deal with the contemplative life, the *Praktikos* confines itself to questions more directly concerned with the active life, with *ascesis*.

However, these various sentences clearly point beyond themselves

---

1. See *Praktikos,* 5. A. Guillaumont in his introduction to Evagrius very well shows the specific contribution made by Evagrius to the concept of *praktike* in the monastic spirituality. Prior to him the term was used in a broader context, of the life of a bishop, for instance, or even of a layman, or a cenobite in a monastery, as contrasted with that of a hermit. This last usage was that of Gregory of Nazianzus. See R. Ruether, *Gregory of Nazianzus: Rhetor and Philosopher* (Oxford, 1969), 138f. Cf. A. and C. Guillaumont, TP 38f.

2. *Letter to Anatolius.*

3. See above, p. lx, concerning the *Gnostikos.*

4. See above, pp. lxf, for a discussion of the *Kephalaia Gnostica.*

G

to the way of contemplation. By their insistence upon *apatheia*[5] which " is the very flower of *ascesis*"[6] and "the health of the soul,"[7] they lead to the threshold of contemplation. For the works of the active life "do not suffice to heal the powers of the soul completely. They must be complemented by a contemplative activity which is appropriate to these faculties . . . ."[8] "Thus it is that we go on eagerly working at the ascetical life so long as we have not tasted this (contemplative) knowledge . . . ."[9]

Since the introduction to Evagrius' theology as a whole has already dealt with the main lines of his system of *ascesis* we shall dwell here only on one further point: the demonology of this treatise.

Of the hundred chapters that make up the *Praktikos,* demons are mentioned in sixty-seven. This preoccupation with the influence of evil spirits on the life of man, and in particular on solitaries, can be a serious obstacle to a twentieth-century reader's appreciation of Evagrius. Paul Valéry has pointedly depicted the attitude that marks modern man's attitude toward demonology. His Faust informs Mephisto that his "reputation in the world is not so grand as it used to be . . ."[10] with a touch of condescending irony that leaves bewildered Mephisto weakly gasping: "No one has ever talked to me this way before." The effect is withering. Such a demon can hardly be taken seriously.

It is no easy thing to bridge the gap between the modern image of a rather pitiable demon, the ineffectual product of backward or weak minds, and the fearsome, powerful and clever spirit whose delight was to inspire terror in the heart of man so as to defeat his every effort to achieve a worthy life.

Long before Evagrius, however, the origins of his demonology were being developed. In Plato, demons occupy a place in the world between the gods and men, acting as intermediaries

---

5. For further details on Evagrius' notion of *apatheia* see above, pp. lxxxiiiff.

6. *Praktikos,* 81.   7. *Ibid.,* 65.

8. *Ibid.,* 79.   9. *Ibid.,* 32.

10. P. Valéry, *Plays,* trans. D. Paul and R. Fitzgerald (New York, 1960), 29.

between these two societies.[11] Plato's demons are all good, rendering various benign services to man, but later on, under the influence, quite probably, of the dualism imported from Iranian culture and possibly Chaldean traditions as well, the Neo-platonists included evil as well as good demons in their world-view and in their religious systems. Elaborate, detailed descriptions of the precise good and evil done by these respective demons became a prominent feature of many of the Neo-platonists' writings. Also specific functions of the pagan cult were intimately associated with these good and evil demons so that pagan religion, in the early Christian centuries, was in fact preoccupied with a whole series of sacrifices to both good and bad demons.

It thus came about that in the period when the first Christian spirituality was being elaborated the early theologians and apologists had to incorporate into their systems of thought a demonology. The world of the demons was, phenomenologically, simply a given fact in the life of man at this period, an important, even crucial fact of experience.

Indeed, in the New Testament it is evident that both good and bad demons were recognized, universally accepted features of the cosmos.[12] The Judeo-Christian theology that represents the most direct continuity with the thought of the New Testament writers eventually gave even more prominence to demonology than the New Testament itself. And this demonology is brought especially into relation with the ascetic life.[13]

There was a ruling concept in the early Church that the ascetic life is a war against demons. The early martyrs viewed their struggle to the death as a contest with the demons whose power was so great that it could be overcome only by the presence of

11. For these views of the development of demonology in antiquity see J. Daniélou, DS, 3:153ff.: "Démon." For the demonology of the classical world see the fine pages of E. R. Dodds, *The Greeks and the Irrational* (Boston, 1957), 28–43.

12. See the thorough study by H. Schlier, *Principalities and Powers in the New Testament* (New York, 1961).

13. J. Daniélou, *The Theology of Jewish Christianity* (London, 1964), 358–362.

Christ in his faithful witness. Likewise the ascetics who under-
took the life of prayer and of ascetic striving after virtue and
spiritual perfection through contemplation viewed their own efforts
as a battle. They understood that attempts to arrive at self-domina-
tion and to grow in perfection means a fight with the demons,
the powers of this world.[14]

Far from being an exception to this view the monks of Egypt
carried it to a further pitch of intensity. It is well known to what an
extent this theme of the combat with demons is operative in the
Life of Anthony by St Athanasius.[15] It is clearly one of the major
theological ideas in this work, that the spiritual life is a combat
against the demonic forces.

Such was the teaching that Evagrius met when he came to Egypt.
He would have learned from his masters, the two Macarii, all the
rich detail of the elaborate demonology that had continued to
evolve since the death of Anthony a generation earlier. It is even
possible that some of the ideas which have been considered to have
come to him from Origen or other Greek influences may well have
actually derived from this Coptic tradition. For instance, there is the
matter of *negligence* that was responsible for the fall away from
unity[16] and which plays an important part too as a continuing
tendency in man's nature. Evagrius may have taken this concept
from a tradition that is expressed in one of the letters of St
Anthony.[17] The same holds true of his view that the angels are
interested in us and do not rest because of us.[18]

Evagrius, however, was to do more than merely accept this

14. Origen in particular developed this view. S. T. Bettencourt, *Doctrina
Ascetica Origenis seu De Ratione Animae Humanae cum Daemonibus* (Rome, 1945).

15. St Athanasius in fact seems to be setting forth what he considers a basic
principle of the spiritual life when he depicts Anthony's advances in the way
of perfection as marked at each stage by increased demonic assaults. ACW,
10:25, 29f.

16. See above, p. lxxv.

17. *Lettres de St Antoine, Version géorgienne et fragments copts,* trans. G.
Garrite, 4:26. Corpus Scriptorum Christianorum Orientalium, 149 (Louvain,
1955), 12.

18. *Ibid.,* 4:98–99, 18f.

tradition. He contributed to it with his analyses and also with the applications he made of this teaching by relating it to his profound psychological insights. The *Praktikos* represents a distinct phase in the evolution of the demonology of the desert tradition. Rather more from the practical side than from elaboration of theories this work makes its contribution to an understanding of the ways and wiles of the various kinds of demons in their assaults upon the ascetic. Future generations would become acquainted with the traditions of the desert concerning these matters largely in the form that they came to assume under the pen of Evagrius.

Rather than attempt to give a complete account of his contribution to this area of asceticism we shall content ourselves with indicating some of the more interesting and original data. The description of the eight *logismoi* is surely the most original and interesting in Evagrius' present work. Not that he necessarily invented the system of eight such evil thoughts,[19] but he has given us a classic description. His abilities as a writer and teacher are clearest in the nine chapters that comprise this section of the *Praktikos*.[20] It would even seem that his reputation in the desert during his own lifetime was based to a large degree upon his analysis and description of these *logismoi*.[21] *The Historia Monachorum in Aegypto* in the brief notice it devotes to Evagrius fastens upon his insight into the workings of the passions as the basis of his reputation for learning and brilliance.[22] The source of this wisdom, it hastens to add, is no mere book knowledge but rather personal experience.

A second point to underline is the fact that the demons influence man through these *logismoi*.[23] This is the reason for devoting so much attention to analyzing the passions.[24] For this insight gives us power,

19. I. Hausherr, "L'origine de la théorie orientale des huit péchés capitaux," *Orientalia Christiana*, 86 (1933), 164–175.

20. Under the section entitled *Eight Kinds of Evil Thoughts*, pp. 16ff.

21. For a good example of this style see also the *Praktikos*, 23–27.

22. A. J. Festugière, *Historia Monachorum in Aegypto*, 20:15, 123.

23. For instance *Praktikos*, 34.

24. *Ibid.*, 43.

Evagrius tells us, anticipating by some thousand years Freud's statements to the same effect.[25] Here are his own words:

> We must take care to recognize the different types of demons and note the special times of their activity . . . so that when these various evil thoughts set their own proper forces to work we are in a position to address effective words against them, that is to say, those words which correctly characterize the one present. . . . In this manner we shall . . . pack them off, chafing with chagrin, marveling at our perspicacity.[26]

Evagrius is well aware of the essential distinction between the demons and the passions. He knows that "the passions are accustomed to be stirred up by the senses."[27] He recognizes that "those memories, colored by passion, that we find in ourselves come from former experiences we underwent while subject to some passion."[28] And still more explicitly: "And so the conqueror of the demons . . . despises not only the demon he conquers, but also these kinds of thoughts he causes in us."[29] Yet he holds that the relation between the demons and the thoughts is extremely close; indeed, his idea of these various demons is that they are each specialists in their own particular field, as it were, by their nature. The demon of vainglory knows all the variations of this most subtle vice, is well practiced in devices and arts by which this thought takes hold of a man, and leads him astray. The same holds true for each of the demons. The key to understanding the nature and quality of the demon is through the most attentive observation of one's inner impulses and thoughts:

> If there is any monk who wishes to take the measure of some of the more fierce demons so as to gain experience in his monastic

25. Insight as the principle for resolving conflicts arising from passion-filled memories and thoughts is the aim of most of the interpretation employed by analysts today, ever since Freud's re-emphasis of this point.

26. *Praktikos*, 43.

27. *Ibid.*, 38. A. Guillaumont points out that, at times, there is an equivalence between the demon and the passionate thought, so that the demon would seem to be the thought hypostatized. Cf. TP, 57.

28. *Ibid.*, 34.   29. *Ibid.*

art, then let him keep careful watch over his thoughts. Let him observe their intensity, their periods of decline, and follow them as they rise and fall. Let him note well the complexity of his thoughts, their periodicity, the demons which cause them, with the order of their succession and the nature of their associations. Then let him ask from Christ the explanations of these data he has observed.[30]

In this view, then, demons represent a source and influence that is distinct from the mere intrinsic psychology of the human soul, a kind of added dimension of the affective life. It also assumes that, though the world of demons is separate from the world of the passions, yet it is in continuity with it, and follows laws analogous to the psychological laws of man's nature.

In view of these data, it would seem that there is a very solid, theologically precise and acceptable basis for Evagrius' demonology, whatever one may choose to think of its practical validity. Further, this theological substructure gives to the majority of his statements concerning demons an air of sobriety and restraint. Lastly, the method of observation employed by Evagrius is as close to a scientific psychology as clinicians are now able to establish. Indeed, the paragraph cited above, except for the reference to demons, reads very much like a practical bit of advice for an intern in clinical psychology. It is the approach of dynamic psychoanalysis with its emphasis on careful observations upon one's most interior and spontaneous thoughts in their risings and fallings, in their associations and relations to one another.

The very last sentence of this same paragraph deserves to be underlined too. "Then let him ask from Christ the explanations of these data he has observed." For Evagrius such observation was a form of searching for God. He simply assumes that Christ would have an interest in assisting such a monk to interpret his findings, for it would obviously be an aid to spiritual growth. Once again there is a profoundly orthodox theology behind such an assumption, a theology that accepts the nature of man in its operations as a sacra-

30. *Ibid.,* 50.

ment of union with Christ. If this point were better appreciated, perhaps there would be less criticism of the tendency of the Desert Fathers generally, and Evagrius in particular, to employ themselves excessively in the understanding of the passions and the heart of man, and insufficiently with the love of God. For them such understanding assured that their love of God was genuine, not based on self-deception or evasion, but on a courageous and humble encounter with the forces of good and evil that aided or barred the way to their ascent. Once the obstacles are removed through intelligent, ascetic effort, directed where insight leads, the grace of Christ will flower fully into a love of God that is ineffable. This is the unexpressed preconception that underlines our author's study of psychology, and his demonology as well. "Put this also to my credit (says Christ), that I preserve you in the desert and put to flight the demons who rage against you."[31]

The Text

This present translation was made from the Greek text printed in Migne *Patrologia Graeca,* 40, which itself is a reproduction of the edition printed in Cotelier, *Ecclesiae Graecae Monumenta,* vol. 3 (1686), 68–102.

However, the state of this text is not altogether satisfactory, especially in regard to the order of the Chapters, as Gennadius himself tells us.[32] In fact he took steps to restore the text. More recently Muyldermans[33] has been able to restore the true order of

31. *Ibid.,* 33. Further evidence for the central place of Christ in Evagrian spirituality is provided in the recently published second half of his "Great Letter" where Evagrius relates the Incarnation, Redemption and Resurrection to the one essential knowledge and finds perfection is hidden "in the breast of Jesus" upon which St John leaned. See G. Vitestam, *Seconde Partie du Traité que Passe sous le Nom de "La Grande Lettre d'Evagre le Pontique à Mélanie l'Ancienne"* (Lund, 1964), 23–29.

32. Gennadius, *op. cit.,* 11 (PL 58:1066).

33. J. Muyldermans, "La teneur du Praktikos d'Evagre le Pontique," *Muséon,* 42 (1929).

the treatise by using the Syriac manuscript tradition, and it is this restored order, the original one, which is followed in this translation.

From the point of view of the readings of the text itself, the Migne edition is surprisingly accurate, as the critical edition, just now completed but not as yet published, reveals. Madame Claire Guillaumont has established the critical text of the *Praktikos* for *Sources Chrétiennes*. She has very generously placed at my disposal all the variants of any significance. Where they differ from the Migne text—they are few indeed—they have been used in this translation. Migne had already noted a number of the variant readings, and these were, even before the work of Madame Guillaumont, evidently the preferred reading in a number of cases. The text of Guillaumont establishes also the same order as that restored by Muyldermans.

For a very thorough and interesting study of the history of the transmission of the text of the *Praktikos*, the study of Guillaumont, to appear shortly in *Sources Chrétiennes,* is very rewarding. It points to the waxing of interest in the work in the eleventh and twelfth centuries when so many of the extant mss were produced.[34]

---

34. The critical text with an introduction was received as the present work was being proofread: A. and C. Guillaumont "Evagre le Pontique, traité pratique ou le moine" (Paris, 1971) (SC 170 and 171). The translation and notes have been most helpful. (Referred to as TP.)

THE PRAKTIKOS

INTRODUCTORY LETTER TO ANATOLIUS[1]

RECENTLY YOU WROTE to me here in Scete, Anatolius my dearest brother, from the Holy Mountain[2] to request from me an explanation of the symbolism of the habit of the monks who live in Egypt.[3] You have well understood that not without purpose is this habit made in a form so very different from what other men employ for the style of their clothes. So let me go on to tell you what I have learned about these matters from the holy Fathers.

1. This introductory letter does not, strictly speaking, form part of the *Praktikos*. In the Syriac tradition it appears at the head of the *Antirrheticos* or the *Protrepticos* and *Paraneticos* (ES, 26). In these notes it is referred to as the *Letter to Anatolius*. Cf. TP, 383 for its relation to the textual history of the Praktikos.

2. What mountain is meant? Possibly Mt Nitria in the Egyptian desert. (This is the opinion given by Theophane the Recluse in his note to this passage *Dobrotolyubie*, 421.) It could also refer to Mt Sinai where there were monks established from very early times. But it may well be a reference to the Mt of Olives where Evagrius had a number of friends with whom he maintained correspondence, chief of whom was Rufinus.

3. On the monastic habit, J. M. Besse, *Les Moines d'Orient antérieurs au Concile de Chalcédoine* (Paris, 1900), 249–54. The symbolism of the monastic habit was influential throughout all the Middle Ages, as Dom Jean Leclercq has pointed out in a personal communication. See *La Vie Parfaite* (Tournhout-Paris, 1948), 20–21 and *passim*. This is probably the first time a symbolic meaning was given to different parts of the habit. Cf. TP, 484.

The cowl is a symbol of the charity of God our Savior. It protects the most important part of the body and keeps us, who are children in Christ, warm. Thus it can be said to afford protection against those who attempt to strike and wound us. Consequently, all who wear this cowl on their heads sing these words aloud: "If the Lord does not build the house and keep the city, unavailingly does the builder labor and the watchman stand his guard."[4] Such words as these instill humility and root out that long-standing evil which is pride and which caused Lucifer, who rose like the day-star in the morning, to be cast down to the earth.[5]

That the monks go with their hands bare is a symbol of a life lived free of all hypocrisy. For vainglory has a frightful power to cover over and cast virtues into the shade. Ever searching out praise from men, it banishes faith. Our Lord has put it very well: "How can you believe when you get your praise from other men and are not interested in the praise that God alone gives?"[6] The good must be pursued for its own sake, not for some other cause. If this is not admitted then it would appear that the occasion that moves us to perform some good deed is better by far than the good that is done. How absurd this is can be seen from the extreme case where one would consider or say that something is better than God.[7]

The scapular which[8] has the form of a cross and which covers the shoulders of the monks is a symbol of faith in Christ which

---

4. Ps 126:1.

5. Lucifer is the Latin name for the day-star. It came to be applied to the Prince of demons very early in the patristic exegesis of Is 14:12 where the literal reference is to a pagan tyrant, probably Sargon II, who had recently died in Assyria. Isaiah describes his death as a well-deserved humiliation of pride.

6. Jn 5:44.

7. Evagrius' thought here is somewhat elliptical. What he leaves out is the statement that to pursue good for some cause other than its own self is precisely what the man does who falls into vainglory. He adds that such a way of acting is manifestly absurd.

8. The Syriac texts adds "which is made of a thin cord and which. . . ." ES, 25.

raises up the meek, removes obstacles[9] and provides for free, untrammeled activity.[10]

The belt which they wear about their loins signifies their rejection of all impurity and proclaims that "it is a good thing for man not to touch a woman."[11] These men, to signify that they continually bear in their bodies the mortification of Jesus[12] and check all the irrational passions, wear also a sheep-skin garment.[13] Further they cut off the vices of the soul by their communion in the good, as also by loving poverty and fleeing from avarice, the mother of idolatry.

They carry a staff which is the tree of life that affords secure footing to those who hold on to it. It allows them to support themselves upon it as upon the Lord.

We see then that the monk's habit is a kind of compendious symbol of all these things we have described. (Whenever they confer this habit) the Fathers speak the following words to the young monks: "The fear of God strengthens faith, my son, and continence in turn strengthens this fear. Patience and hope make this latter virtue solid beyond all shaking and they also give birth to *apatheia*.[14] Now this *apatheia* has a child called *agape* who keeps the door to deep knowledge of the created universe.[15] Finally, to this knowledge succeed theology and the supreme beatitude."[16]

Let this suffice then for our explanation of the meaning of the holy habit and for the teaching of the ancients, and now let us go on to the discussion of the ways of the ascetic and contemplative lives. We shall not, to be sure, tell everything that we have seen or heard, but as much as we have been taught by the Fathers to tell

9. The Syriac text adds "from their monastic life; and thus this cord. . . ."; *ibid*.

10. Cassian gives a more precise description of the scapular. Cf. J. C. Guy, "Jean Cassien, institutions cenobitiques" (Paris, 1965), SC 109:45–7.

11. 1 Cor 7:1.   12. 2 Cor 4:10.

13. The sheep here is seen as a symbol of sacrifice, the reference being to the Paschal lamb and to the sheep spoken of in Is 53:7.

14. For *apatheia* see pp. lxxxiiiff above.

15. For the relation between *agape* and *apatheia* see p. lxxxii above.

16. This paragraph gives a succinct summary of the spiritual life according to Evagrius. While the individual ideas it contains are all quite traditional, the particular manner of relating them is quite original with the author.

to others.[17] We shall make a concise distribution of the material into one hundred chapters on the ascetic life[18] and fifty plus another six hundred on contemplative matters. So as "not to give what is holy to the dogs or to cast our pearls before swine" some of these matters will be kept in concealment and others alluded to only obscurely, but yet so as to keep them quite clear to those who walk along in the same path.[19]

THE HUNDRED CHAPTERS[20]

1. Christianity is the dogma of Christ our Savior. It is composed of *praktike*, of the contemplation of the physical world and of the contemplation of God.[21]

2. The Kingdom of Heaven is *apatheia* of the soul along with true knowledge of existing things.[22]

17. Evagrius gives special importance to the duty of the spiritual master to conceal such points of doctrine as were beyond the powers or merits of the disciple. But he shared this practice with the other great theologians of the Patristic Age.

18. These one hundred chapters on the ascetic life comprise the *Praktikos*. The fifty chapters referred to make up the *Gnostikos*, while the six hundred chapters are the *Kephalaia Gnostica*. This, the *Praktikos*, is the first part of a trilogy.

19. See also PG 40:1285B where Evagrius again asserts this principle.

20. The Guillaumonts have shown that the rubric directing scribes to copy each chapter separately probably goes back to Evagrius himself. It is found in a number of mss: TP 384f. The titles of the sections of chapters also seem to be from Evagrius. Cf. TP 116f.

21. This chapter formulates very concisely the teaching of Clement of Alexandria and of Origen, as I. Hausherr indicates in his article on "Les grands courants de la spiritualité orientale," OCP, 1 (1935), 121. A. Guillaumont, in his introduction to the works of Evagrius soon to appear in SC will show that it was Evagrius who introduced the concept of *praktike* into the monastic vocabulary. In earlier periods it was employed with another meaning and in another context. Gregory Nazianzen, for instance, used it to describe the life of a bishop. Cf. TP 83f.

22. γνῶις τῶν ὄντων ἀληθής is an expression which refers to the activity of θεωρία φυσική by which man knows God indirectly through his creation. Note

3. The Kingdom of God is knowledge of the Holy Trinity co-extensive with the capacity of the intelligence and giving it a surpassing incorruptibility.

4. Whatever a man loves he will desire with all his might. What he desires he strives to lay hold of. Now desire precedes every pleasure, and it is feeling which gives birth to desire. For that which is not subject to feeling is also free of passion.[23]

5. The demons fight openly against the solitaries, but they arm the more careless of the brethren against the cenobites, or those who practice virtue in the company of others. Now this second form of combat is much lighter than the first, for there is not to be found on earth any men more fierce than the demons, none who support at the same time all their evil deeds.

THE EIGHT KINDS OF EVIL THOUGHTS[24]

6. There are eight general and basic categories of thoughts in which are included every thought. First is that of gluttony, then

that Evagrius makes a distinction between the Kingdom of Heaven and the Kingdom of God, basing the distinction upon the type of contemplation engaged in by the believer. Cassian, however, did not maintain this distinction. See the remarks by G. Colombás, *op. cit.*, 299, note 258. It is interesting to compare the concept of *true gnosis* of *beings* with the Hindu contemplation of the *tattva* (essence) of objects. The parallels with Hindu psychology and ascesis are striking. See M. Eliade, *Yoga. Immortality and Freedom*, trans. W. R. Trask, 2nd ed. (New York, 1969), 69.

23. Feeling, αἴσθησις, is for Evagrius an "accidental faculty" which has its seat in the psyche. It is here considered in its negative aspect as the fruit of sin. And indeed in the Evagrian conception all the powers of the affective part of man are, indirectly, the result of sin. But for Evagrius this faculty of αἴσθησις has a more positive side too as is revealed, for instance, in the *Chapters on Prayer*, 41 and 42 (in the Philokalia· text) and in 98 as well. The reference is to the sense (αἴσθησις) of prayer.

24. This section dealing with the eight capital vices is printed in Migne as a separate work, but Muyldermans has shown that these chapters form an integral part of the *Praktikos*, being inserted by Evagrius himself, en bloc, after chapter five of this work.

impurity, avarice, sadness, anger, *acedia,* vainglory, and last of all, pride. It is not in our power to determine whether we are disturbed by these thoughts, but it is up to us to decide if they are to linger within us or not and whether or not they are to stir up our passions.

7. The thought of gluttony suggests to the monk that he give up his ascetic efforts in short order. It brings to his mind concern for his stomach, for his liver and spleen, the thought of a long illness, scarcity of the commodities of life and finally of his edematous body and the lack of care by the physicians. These things are depicted vividly before his eyes. It frequently brings him to recall certain ones among the brethren who have fallen upon such sufferings. There even comes a time when it persuades those who suffer from such maladies to visit those who are practicing a life of abstinence and to expose their misfortune and relate how these came about as a result of the ascetic life.

8. The demon of impurity impels one to lust after bodies. It attacks more strenuously those who practice continence, in the hope that they will give up their practice of this virtue, feeling that they gain nothing by it. This demon has a way of bowing the soul down to practices of an impure kind, defiling it, and causing it to speak and hear certain words almost as if the reality were actually present to be seen.

9. Avarice suggests to the mind a lengthy old age, inability to perform manual labor (at some future date), famines that are sure to come, sickness that will visit us, the pinch of poverty, the great shame that comes from accepting the necessities of life from others.

10. Sadness tends to come up at times because of the deprivations of one's desires. On other occasions it accompanies anger. When it arises from the deprivation of desires it takes place in the following manner. Certain thoughts first drive the soul to the memory of home and parents, or else to that of one's former life. Now when these thoughts find that the soul offers no resistance but

rather follows after them and pours itself out in pleasures that are still only mental in nature, they then seize her and drench her in sadness, with the result that these ideas she was just indulging no longer remain. In fact they cannot be had in reality, either, because of her present way of life. So the miserable soul is now shriveled up in her humiliation to the degree that she poured herself out upon these thoughts of hers.

11. The most fierce passion is anger. In fact it is defined as a boiling and stirring up of wrath against one who has given injury— or is thought to have done so. It constantly irritates the soul and above all at the time of prayer it seizes the mind and flashes the picture of the offensive person before one's eyes. Then there comes a time when it persists longer, is transformed into indignation, stirs up alarming experiences by night. This is succeeded by a general debility of the body, malnutrition with its attendant pallor, and the illusion of being attacked by poisonous wild beasts. These four last mentioned consequences following upon indignation may be found to accompany many thoughts.[25]

12. The demon of *acedia*—also called the noonday demon[26]— is the one that causes the most serious trouble of all. He presses his attack upon the monk about the fourth hour and besieges the soul until the eighth hour. First of all he makes it seem that the sun barely moves, if at all, and that the day is fifty hours long. Then he constrains the monk to look constantly out the windows, to walk outside the cell, to gaze carefully at the sun to determine how far it stands from the ninth hour,[27] to look now this way and now that to

25. This interesting description of the dynamics of disproportionate anger will be appreciated for its accuracy perhaps only by those who have carefully followed the progression of certain forms of schizophrenia.

26. On the origins of this term "noonday demon" see note 43 below. For a discussion of the originality and significance of Evagrius' concept of acedia see the article by S. Wenzel, "'Ακηδία. Additions to Lampe's *Patristic Greek Lexicon*," *Vigiliae Christianae*, 17 (1963), 173–76.

27. The ninth hour (3 PM) was the usual hour for dinner.

see if perhaps [one of the brethren appears from his cell].²⁸ Then too
he instills in the heart of the monk a hatred for the place, a hatred
for his very life itself, a hatred for manual labor. He leads him to
reflect that charity has departed from among the brethren, that there
is no one to give encouragement. Should there be someone at this
period who happens to offend him in some way or other, this too
the demon uses to contribute further to his hatred. This demon
drives him along to desire other sites where he can more easily
procure life's necessities, more readily find work and make a real
success of himself. He goes on to suggest that, after all, it is not the
place that is the basis of pleasing the Lord. God is to be adored
everywhere. He joins to these reflections the memory of his dear
ones and of his former way of life. He depicts life stretching out for
a long period of time, and brings before the mind's eye the toil of
the ascetic struggle and, as the saying has it, leaves no leaf unturned
to induce the monk to forsake his cell and drop out of the fight. No
other demon follows close upon the heels of this one (when he is
defeated) but only a state of deep peace and inexpressible joy arise
out of this struggle.²⁹

13. The spirit of vainglory is most subtle and it readily grows
up in the souls of those who practice virtue. It leads them to desire
to make their struggles known publicly, to hunt after the praise
of men. This in turn leads to their illusory healing of women, or
to their hearing fancied sounds as the cries of the demons—crowds
of people who touch their clothes. This demon predicts besides
that they will attain to the priesthood. It has men knocking at the
door, seeking audience with them. If the monk does not willingly
yield to their request, he is bound and led away. When in this way

28. Guillaumont, TP, 455f. shows that the elipsis is deliberate and stylistic
for Evagrius.

29. This deep peace accompanied by joy characterizes the *apatheia* of
Evagrius. But, as the next two chapters reveal, this state still admits of further
assaults from the passion under the influence of demons. This is important to
note as a response to those who criticized Evagrius for demanding an un-
natural control of the passions, a complete extirpation as it were, as the basic
state required for a serious contemplative life.

H

he is carried aloft by vain hope, the demon vanishes and the monk is left to be tempted by the demon of pride or of sadness who brings upon him thoughts opposed to his hopes. It also happens at times that a man who a short while before was a holy priest, is led off bound and is handed over to the demon of impurity to be sifted by him.[30]

14. The demon of pride is the cause of the most damaging fall for the soul. For it induces the monk to deny that God is his helper and to consider that he himself is the cause of virtuous actions. Further, he gets a big head in regard to the brethren, considering them stupid because they do not all have this same opinion of him.

Anger and sadness follow on the heels of this demon, and last of all there comes in its train the greatest of maladies—derangement of mind, associated with wild ravings and hallucinations of whole multitudes of demons in the sky.[31]

AGAINST THE EIGHT PASSIONATE THOUGHTS

15. Reading, vigils and prayer—these are the things that lend stability to the wandering mind. Hunger, toil and solitude are the means of extinguishing the flames of desire. Turbid anger is calmed by the singing of Psalms, by patience and almsgiving. But all these practices are to be engaged in according to due measure and at the appropriate times. What is untimely done, or done without measure, endures but a short time. And what is short-lived is more harmful than profitable.

30. This chapter should be read in conjunction with chapter 31 where Evagrius speaks of the advantages of knowing the specific qualities of the various demonic attacks. Evagrius is persuaded, quite correctly, that knowledge of these data would prove reassuring as well as directly helpful in defensive tactics.

31. Budge gives a number of instances of various monks who fell into the trap of pride where the description is obviously modeled on the "type" given here. An instance is that of the monk Stephana. See Budge, *op. cit.,* 401–403.

16. When the soul desires to seek after a variety of foods then it is time to afflict it with bread and water that it may learn to be grateful for a mere morsel of bread. For satiety desires a variety of dishes but hunger thinks itself happy to get its fill of nothing more than bread.[32]

17. Limiting one's intake of water helps a great deal to obtain temperance. This was well understood by the three hundred Israelites accompanying Gideon just when they were preparing to attack Midian.[33]

18. Just as death and life cannot be shared in at the same time, so also is it an impossibility for charity to exist in anyone along with money. For charity not only gets rid of money but even of this present life itself.

19. The man who flees from all worldly pleasures is an impregnable tower before the assaults of the demon of sadness. For sadness is a deprivation of sensible pleasure, whether actually present or only hoped for. And so if we continue to cherish some affection for anything in this world it is impossible to repel this enemy, for he lays his snares and produces sadness precisely where he sees we are particularly inclined.

20. Both anger and hatred increase anger. But almsgiving and meekness diminish it even when it is present.

21. Let not the sun go down upon our anger lest by night the demons come upon us to strike fear in our souls and render our spirits more cowardly for the fight on the morrow. For images of a

---

32. St John Climachus selects this bit of advice from the Evagrian writings to indicate how fully he was deceived by pride (*op. cit.,* 14:12, p. 141). It is a curious comment on the prejudice to which he was subject regarding Evagrius that he chose to criticize so harshly a very minor point, which, after all, is based on a valid observation of experience and is not even an interpretation.

33. Judg 7:5-6.

frightful kind usually arise from anger's disturbing influence. Indeed, there is nothing more disposed to render the spirit inclined to desertion than troubled irascibility.[34]

22. When under some provocation or other the irascible part of our soul is stirred up, it is just at that moment that the demons suggest to us the advantages of solitude so as to have us deliver ourselves from the disturbance rather than clear up the basic causes of the sadness. When it is our lust that flames up they cause us to seek out once again the friendly company of men and call us callous and uncivil in the hope that while we feel the desire for bodies we might happen upon them. But give no confidence to such promptings; on the contary, follow the opposite course.[35]

23. Do not give yourself over to your angry thoughts so as to fight in your mind with the one who has vexed you. Nor again to thoughts of fornication, imagining the pleasure vividly. The one darkens the soul; the other invites to the burning of passion. Both cause your mind to be defiled and while you indulge these fancies at the time of prayer, and thus do not offer pure prayer to God, the demon of *acedia*[36] falls upon you without delay. He falls above all

---

34. Was the keen awareness Evagrius had of the evil consequences of anger in all its varied forms (resentment, hatred and, when inverted, sadness and depression) based solely on his experiences with men and knowledge of himself? Or was he also impressed with the place of anger in classical Greek literature, and especially in Homer? "Anger that is far sweeter than trickling honey and grows in men's hearts like smoke—anger that makes even the prudent take offense." *The Iliad,* 18, 108–110, trans. W. Rouse (New York, 1950), 218. But also in the Stoics. Cf. TP, 551.

35. This program of dealing with temptations and difficulties by application of opposites is a favorite of Evagrius. Besides the instance in c. 7 above, there is the whole of the *Antirrheticos.* This principle may well have come from the Greek physicians who employed it in their medical practice. We know that St Basil, who first formed Evagrius in the spiritual life, gave considerable space to medical theories in his ascetic teaching, as is evident for instance in Question 55 of his Long Rules: "Whether recourse to medical art is in keeping with the practice of piety?" *St Basil Ascetical Works,* trans., A. Way (Washington, 1950), 330–37.

36. ἀκηδία is the most fierce of all the demons. See c. 12 above.

upon souls in this state and, dog-like, snatches away the soul as if it were a fawn.

24. Anger is given to us so that we might fight against the demons and strive against every pleasure. Now it happens that the angels suggest spiritual pleasure to us and the beatitude that is consequent upon it so as to encourage us to turn our anger against the demons. But these, for their part, draw our anger to worldly desires and constrain us—contrary to our nature—to fight against our fellow men to the end that, blinded in mind and falling away from knowledge, our spirit should become a traitor to virtue.

25. Be very attentive lest ever you cause some brother to become a fugitive through your anger. For if this should happen your whole life long you will yourself not be able to flee from the demon of sadness. At the time of prayer this will be a constant stumbling-block to you.

26. A gift snuffs out the fire of resentment, as Jacob well knew. For he flattered Esau with gifts when he went out to meet him with four hundred men. But as for ourselves who are poor men we must supply for our lack of gifts by the table we lay.[37]

27. When we meet with the demon of *acedia* then is the time with tears to divide our soul in two. One part is to encourage; the other is to be encouraged. Thus we are to sow seeds of a firm hope in ourselves while we sing with the holy David: "Why are you filled with sadness, my soul? Why are you distraught? Trust in God, for I shall give praise to him. He it is who saves me, the light of my eyes and my God."[38]

---

37. His thought here is again elliptical. Does Evagrius mean to say that by fasting we shall be able to save enough money to give some gift to another? Or that by fasting we appease God's just anger toward us? Either would suit the context. The reference here is to Gen 32:15.

38. Ps 41:6–7. The Psalms are cited according to the Vulgate enumeration.

28. The time of temptation is not the time to leave one's cell, devising plausible pretexts. Rather, stand there firmly and be patient. Bravely take all that the demon brings upon you, but above all face up to the demon of *acedia* who is the most grievous of all and who on this account will effect the greatest purification of soul. Indeed to flee and to shun such conflicts schools the spirit in awkwardness, cowardice and fear.

29. Our holy and most ascetic master[39] stated that the monk should always live as if he were to die on the morrow but at the same time that he should treat his body as if he were to live on with it for many years to come. For, he said, by the first attitude he will be able to cut off every thought that comes from *acedia*[40] and thus become more fervent in his monastic practices, by the second device he will preserve his body in good health and maintain its continence intact.

30. It is only with considerable difficulty that one can escape the thought of vainglory. For what you do to destroy it becomes the principle of some other form of vainglory. Now the demons do not oppose every good thought of ours, the vices which we have also oppose some of them.[41]

31. I have observed the demon of vainglory being chased by nearly all the other demons, and when his pursuers fell, shamelessly he drew near and unfolded a long list of his virtues.

32. When a man has once attained to contemplative knowledge and the delight that derives from it he will no longer yield himself

39. The reference is to Macarius the Great. For a similar idea on the care of the body see Nau, "Histoires des solitaires égyptiens," *Rev. d'Or. Chr.,* 13 (1908) 66, # 71.

40. *Acedia* is such a complex reality and the term has such a technical significance for the system of Evagrius that it seems best always to retain it without translation.

41. Cf. TP 571 for a discussion of this chapter.

up to the demon of vainglory, though the demon offer all the delights of the world to him. For what, may I ask, could surpass spiritual contemplation? Thus it is that we go on eagerly working at the ascetical life so long as we have not tasted this knowledge, proving to God that we do everything for the sole aim of attaining it.

33. Remember your former life and your past sins and how, though you were subject to the passions, you have been brought into *apatheia* by the mercy of Christ. Remember too how you have separated yourself from the world which has so often and in so many matters brought you low. "Put this also to my credit (says Christ) that I preserve you in the desert and put to flight the demons who rage against you." Such thoughts instill humility in us and afford no entrance to the demon of pride.

34. Those memories, colored by passion, that we find in ourselves come from former experiences we underwent while subject to some passion. Whatever experience we now undergo while under the influence of passion will in the future persist in us in the form of passionate memories. And so the conqueror of the demons, who are the ones who cause this sort of thing in us, despises not only the demon he conquers, but also these kinds of thoughts he causes in us. For, be sure of it, the immaterial enemy is more fierce than the material one (that is, the passionate thought).

35. The passions of the soul are occasioned by men. Those of the body come from the body. Now the passions of the body are cut off by continence and those of the soul by spiritual love.[42]

36. The demons that rule over the passions of the soul persevere until death. Those which rule over the bodily passions depart more

---

42. Vainglory is an example of a "passion of the soul"; pride, *acedia,* avarice and probably anger are also in this category. This emphasis on spiritual love as the remedy for these passions is a highly significant indication of the relations between *apatheia* and *agape.* Purification of passions supposes love. Love fully flowers only when the passions are put in order.

quickly. The other demons are like the rising or setting sun in that they are found in only a part of the soul. The noonday demon,[43] however, is accustomed to embrace the entire soul and oppress the spirit. It is therefore after the extinction of the passions that the solitary life is sweet, for then the memories are only simple. The struggle, moreover, prepares the monk, not for a fight itself but rather for the contemplation of the fight.

37. Let us broach the question of whether the thought causes the passions or the passions cause the thought, for some have held to the first view and others to the second.

38. The passions are accustomed to be stirred up by the senses, so that when charity and continence are lodged in the soul then the passions are not stirred up. And when they are absent the passions are stirred up. Anger stands more in need of remedies than concupiscence and for that reason the love that is charity is to be reckoned a great thing indeed in that it is able to bridle anger. The great and holy man Moses, where he treats of the things of nature, refers to it symbolically as the killer of snakes.[44]

39. The psyche will usually flare up against the passionate thoughts at the evil smell of the demons, who are perceived as they draw near and affect the soul with the passion of its assailants.

---

43. The noonday demon is the demon of *acedia* as seen in c. 12 above. The name is derived from the text of Ps 90:6 (in the Vulgate and Septuagint readings; the Hebrew has "The deadly disease striking at noon"). It is applied to *acedia* because this affliction comes upon the monk commonly at midday. For a detailed discussion of the Fathers on this passage see the interesting article by R. Arbesmann, "The 'Demonium Meridianum' and Greek Patristic Exegesis," *Traditio,* 14 (1958), 17–31.

44. Lev 11:22 (Septuagint; the Hebrew refers to a type of locust, rendered by the Septuagint ὀφιομάχης, literally destroyer of snakes). In any case it seems altogether arbitrary to find in this text a symbol of charity, but the early fathers took delight and edification in such agile wordplay.

INSTRUCTIONS

40. One is not always in a position to follow his usual rule of life but one must always be on the alert to seize the opportunities to fulfill all the duties possible to the best of his powers. The demons are not ignorant of the possibilities offered them on such occasions. Thus it happens that in their passion against us they prevent our fulfilling what is possible and constrain us to undertake things that are impossible for us. They prevent the sick from giving thanks while undergoing pain and from bearing patiently with the various ministrations they require. Again they encourage the weak to feats of fasting and those who are weighed down with illness to sing standing on their feet for prolonged periods.

41. When we are constrained to pass some time in the city or town then above all is the time to be abstemious. We find ourselves in the presence of secular persons and this measure will prevent the edge of our spirit from being dulled. We shall be able to avoid perpetrating some ill-considered action which being temporarily deprived of our customary practices we might be led to commit. Under the demons' assaults such action might cause us to take flight from our monastic practices altogether.

42. When you are tempted do not fall immediately to prayer. First utter some angry words against the one who afflicts you. The reason for this is found in the fact that your soul cannot pray purely when it is under the influence of various thoughts. By first speaking out in anger against them you confound and bring to nothing the devices of the enemy. To be sure this is the usual effect of anger even upon more worthy thoughts.[45]

45. For a discussion of Evagrius' keen awareness of the harm done to prayer by anger in its various manifestations and effects, see the *Chapters on Prayer,*

43. We must take care to recognize the different types of demons and take note of the circumstances of their coming. We shall know these from our thoughts (which we shall know from the objects) we ought to consider which of the demons are less frequent in their assaults, which are the more vexatious, which are the ones which yield the field more readily and which the more resistant. Finally we should note which are the ones which make sudden raids and snatch off the spirit to blasphemy. Now it is essential to understand these matters so that when these various evil thoughts set their own proper forces to work we are in a position to address effective words against them, that is to say, those words which correctly characterize the one present. And we must do this before they drive us out of our own state of mind. In this manner we shall make ready progress, by the grace of God. We shall pack them off chafing with chagrin and marvelling at our perspicacity.

44. When the demons achieve nothing in their struggles against a monk they withdraw a bit and observe to see which of the virtues he neglects in the meantime. Then all of a sudden they attack him from this point and ravage the poor fellow.

45. The depraved demons attract to their assistance other demons more depraved than themselves and while they agree solely upon the destruction of the soul, they contend among themselves for the various affections.

46. Let us not be upset by that demon who snatches away the intelligence to blasphemy and to those phantasies of a prohibited sort—too sordid to so much as mention. Nor should we let him

---

cc. 20–27. This technique for resisting temptation is the principle behind the book Evagrius entitled *Antirrheticus*. He provides specific sayings against each of the major vices. Though this approach has been sharply criticized, yet there is a very real value in it, at least to this extent that sharp identification of the precise nature of our thoughts gives us a decided advantage in our efforts to work with or against them as the case may be. This is a cardinal principle of modern psychoanalytic work.

dull our sharp eagerness. Remember this, "the Lord knows the heart," and he well knows that even when we were living in the world we did not fall into this kind of madness. The fact is that this demon entertains the hope of causing us to cease to pray so that we might not stand in the presence of the Lord our God, not dare to raise our hands in supplication to one against whom we have had such frightful thoughts.

47. The spoken word or some movement made by the body is a sign of the passions of the soul. By means of such signs our enemies perceive whether we have conceived their thought within us and bring it forth or, on the contrary, through concern for our salvation cast it away. It is God alone, who has created us, who knows our spirits. He has no need of a sign to discover the secrets in our hearts.

48. The demons strive against men of the world chiefly through their deeds, but in the case of monks for the most part by means of thoughts, since the desert deprives them of such affairs. Just as it is easier to sin by thought than by deed, so also is the war fought on the field of thought more severe than that which is conducted in the area of things and events. For the mind is easily moved indeed, and hard to control in the presence of sinful phantasies.

49. We have received no command to work and to pass the night in vigils and to fast constantly. However, we do have the obligation to pray without ceasing. Although the body, due to its weakness, does not suffice for such labors as these, which are calculated to restore health to the passionate part of the soul, these practices do require the body for their performance. But prayer makes the spirit strong and pure for combat since by its very nature the spirit is made to pray. Moreover, prayer even fights without the aid of the body on behalf of the other powers of the soul.

50. If there is any monk who wishes to take the measure of some of the more fierce demons so as to gain experience in his monastic art, then let him keep careful watch over his thoughts. Let him

observe their intensity, their periods of decline and follow them as they rise and fall. Let him note well the complexity of his thoughts, their periodicity, the demons which cause them, with the order of their succession and the nature of their associations. Then let him ask from Christ the explanations of these data he has observed. For the demons become thoroughly infuriated with those who practice active virtue in a manner that is increasingly contemplative. They are even of a mind to "pierce the upright of heart through, under cover of darkness."[46]

51. Watch carefully and you will discover the two swiftest demons—they are nearly more swift than the speed of thought. Their names: the demon of impurity and the demon of blasphemy against God. Now this latter's attack has a short life-span, and the former will be unable to stand in the way of our contemplation of God if he is unable to stir up in us thoughts filled with passion.

52. To separate the body from the soul is the privilege only of the One who has joined them together. But to separate the soul from the body lies as well in the power of the man who pursues virtue. For our Fathers gave to the meditation of death and to the flight from the body a special name: *anachoresis.*[47]

53. Those who give but scant nourishment to their bodies and yet "take thought for the flesh to satisfy its lusts"[48] have only themselves to blame and not their bodies. For those who have attained to purity of heart by means of the body and who in some measure

---

46. Ps 10:3.

47. ἀναχώρησις means literally *withdrawal.* But very early it became a technical expression to indicate the monastic life. The expression "flight from the body" has somewhat odious overtones to modern ears, and needs to be seen in relation to the whole elaborate system for direct confrontation with the passions in order to interpret what it meant to Evagrius. It was far from being an evasion or denial, though it is certainly related to the Neo-platonic world-view.

48. Rom 13:14.

have applied themselves to the contemplation of created things know the grace of the Creator (in giving them a body).

54. The demons wage a veritable war against our concupiscible appetite. They employ for this combat phantasms (and we run to see them) which show conversations with our friends, banquets with our relatives, whole choruses of women and all kinds of other things calculated to produce delight. Under the influence of this part of our soul we then grow unhealthy while our passions undergo a full-bodied development. When, on another occasion, the demons stimulate the irascible appetite they constrain us to walk along precipitous paths where they have us encounter armed men, poisonous snakes and man-eating beasts. We are filled with terror before such sights, and fleeing we are pursued by the beasts and the armed men. Let us make provision for protecting this power of our soul by praying to Christ in our nightly vigils, and also by applying the remedies we spoke of above.[49]

55. Natural processes which occur in sleep without accompanying images of a stimulating nature are, to a certain measure, indications of a healthy soul. But images that are distinctly formed are a clear indication of sickness. You may be certain that the faces one sees in dreams are, when they occur as ill-defined images, symbols of former affective experiences. Those which are seen clearly, on the other hand, indicate wounds that are still fresh.[50]

56. We recognize the indications of *apatheia* by our thoughts during the day, but we recognize it by our dreams during the night. We call *apatheia* the health of the soul. The food of the soul can be said to be contemplative knowledge since it alone is able to unite us with the holy powers. This holds true since union between incorporeal beings follows quite naturally from their sharing the same deep attitudes.

49. Evagrius refers to such passages as *Praktikos* 20, 22, etc.
50. This is another instance of Evagrius' accurate observation of dream dynamics.

THE STATE BORDERING ON *APATHEIA*

57. There are two peaceful states of the soul.[51] The one arises from the natural basic energies of the soul and the other from the withdrawal of the demons. Humility together with compunction and tears, longing for the Infinite God, and a boundless eagerness for toil—all these follow upon the first type. But it is vainglory along with pride that succeeds to the second type, and these lure the monk along as the other demons withdraw from him. The monk who preserves intact the territory of the first state will perceive with greater sensitivity the raids made upon it by the demons.

58. The demon of vainglory lives in a state of opposition to the demon of impurity, so that it is not possible for both of them to assault the soul at the same time. For the one promises honors while the other becomes the agent of dishonor. And so whichever of these two draws near to harass you, feign that the thoughts of the other antagonist is present within you.[52] Should you then be able, as the saying has it, to drive out a nail with a nail, you can know for certain that you stand near the confines of *apatheia,* for your mind is strong enough to abolish thoughts inspired by the demons with human thoughts. Beyond any doubt, the ability to drive away the thought of vainglory through humility, or the power to repel the demon of impurity through temperance is a most profound proof of *apatheia.* Make every attempt to deal in this same way with all the demons that are mutually opposed to one another. At the same time learn to recognize by which emotion you are more inclined to be led astray, and employ your whole strength in pleading with God to ward off your enemies in this second manner also.

51. "State of soul" translates the Greek κατάστασις, an important technical term for Evagrius. It implies a certain fixed degree of perfection and a quality of peace that extends even into the unconscious.

52. This procedure has always seemed to most spiritual directors an imprudent one. See, for instance, Barsanuphius cited by W. Völker, *Scala Paradisi* (Wiesbaden, 1968), 69. The indirect approach to overcoming such thoughts is favored. Evagrius in fact recommends it only to the advanced.

59. The greater the progress the soul makes the more fearful the adversaries that take over the war against her. I do not accept the opinion that the same demons always remain about her.[53] Those who fall into more severe temptations above all know the truth of this view, for they observe that the measure of purity of heart they have achieved is worked over by successive demons.

60. Perfect purity of heart develops in the soul after the victory over all the demons whose function it is to offer opposition to the ascetic life. But there is designated an imperfect purity of heart in consideration of the power of the demon that meantime fights against it.

61. The spirit would not make progress nor go forth on that happy sojourn with the band of the incorporeal beings unless it should correct its interior. This is so because anxiety arising from interior conflicts is calculated to turn it back upon the things that it has left behind.

62. Both the virtues and the vices make the mind blind. The one so that it may not see the vices; the other, in turn, so that it might not see the virtues.

ON THE SIGNS OF *APATHEIA*

63. When the spirit begins to be free from all distractions as it makes its prayer then there commences an all-out battle day and night against the irascible part.

64. The proof of *apatheia* is had when the spirit begins to see its own light, when it remains in a state of tranquility in the presence

53. In the *Shepherd Hermas* is found the teaching that each man has a proper demon assigned to tempt him. Although Origen and other theologians took up this concept it never found general acceptance in tradition. Cf. *Hermas le Pasteur*, trans. et ed. R. Joly SC 53 (Paris, 1958), 172.

of the images it has during sleep[54] and when it maintains its calm as it beholds the affairs of life.

65. The spirit that possesses health is the one which has no images of the things of this world at the time of prayer.

66. The spirit that is actively leading the ascetic life with God's help and which draws near to contemplative knowledge ceases to perceive the irrational part of the soul almost completely, perhaps altogether. For this knowledge bears it aloft and separates it from the senses.[55]

67. The soul which has *apatheia* is not simply the one which is not disturbed by changing events but the one which remains unmoved at the memory of them as well.

68. The perfect man does not work at remaining continent, nor does the man with *apatheia* work at being patient. For patience is the virtue of a man who experiences untoward emotions and continence is the virtue of a man who suffers disturbing impulses.[56]

54. Evagrius had a remarkable knowledge of dream-psychology which presents many points of comparison with modern dynamic theories and observations. See the detailed discussion in F. Refoulé, "Rêves et Vie Spirituelle d'après Evagre le Pontique," *La Vie Spirituelle Supplément,* 14 (1961), 470–516. This very important remark about "the spirit seeing its own light" is of great interest in the psychology of mystical experience. M. Eliade has pointed out some of its relevance for Hindu spirituality where, for instance, "concentration of the 'lotus of the heart' " leads to an experience of pure light. He observes that "the light of the heart" is often encountered in the mystical doctrine of the post-Upanishads and always in the context of encountering the true self. M. Eliade, *Yoga* (New York, 1969), 70. The role of this concept of the inner light in Byzantine spirituality would seem to have been considerable.

55. Not in the sense of leading to an ecstasy but rather in the sense of establishing it in the higher spiritual awareness as a more or less permanent state. Ecstasy plays no formal part in Evagrian spirituality. As I. Hausherr points out it does not occur in his writings except in the sense of "madness." See "Les grands courants de spiritualité orientale," *OCP,* 1 (1935), 125, n. 1.

56. That is, the patience of the perfect man is beyond patience, as it were, so steady has his natural condition become.

69. A great thing indeed—to pray without distraction; a greater thing still—to sing psalms without distraction.

70. A man who has established the virtues in himself and is entirely permeated with them no longer remembers the law or commandments or punishment. Rather, he says and does what excellent habit suggests.

71. The songs inspired by the demons incite our desire and plunge our soul into shameful fancies. But "psalms and hymns and spiritual canticles" invite the spirit to the constant memory of virtue by cooling our boiling anger and by extinguishing our lusts.

72. Wrestlers are not the only ones whose occupation it is to throw others down and to be thrown in turn; the demons too wrestle—with us. Sometimes they throw us and at other times it is we who throw them. For, "I shall crush them," says the Psalmist, "and they shall be unable to stand."[57] Again, "Those who throw me down, and who are my enemies are themselves made weak and fall."[58]

73. Repose is yoked with wisdom and labor with prudence. Wisdom is not won except by a battle, nor is the battle well fought except with prudence. To this prudence is entrusted the fight against the fury of the demons. It achieves this end and thus prepares the way for wisdom by constraining all the powers of the soul to operate according to their nature.

74. Temptation is the lot of the monk, for thoughts which darken his mind will inevitably arise from the part of his soul that is the seat of passion.

75. The sin that a monk has particularly to watch out for is that of giving mental consent to some forbidden pleasure.

57. Ps 17:39.   58. Ps 26:2.

ɪ

76. When evil is made to decrease it is the angels who rejoice; when it is virtue that diminishes it is the turn of the demons to be happy. These former are the ministers of mercy and charity; the latter are servants of anger and hatred. The angels when they draw near us fill us with spiritual contemplation; the demons inspire shameful images in our soul.

77. Virtues do not prevent the demons from assaulting us, but they do preserve us guiltless.

78. The ascetic life is the spiritual method for cleansing the affective part of the soul.

79. The effects of keeping the commandments do not suffice to heal the powers of the soul completely. They must be complemented by a contemplative activity appropriate to these faculties and this activity must penetrate the spirit.

80. It is not possible to resist all the thoughts inspired in us by the angels, though we can indeed overthrow all those inspired by the demons. A peaceful state follows the first kind of thoughts; turbulence of mind attends the second type.

81. *Agape* is the progeny of *apatheia*. *Apatheia* is the very flower of *ascesis*. *Ascesis* consists in keeping the commandments. The custodian of these commandments is the fear of God which is in turn the offspring of true faith. Now faith is an interior good, one which is to be found even in those who do not yet believe in God.[59]

82. Just as the soul perceives its sick members as it operates by means of the body, so also the spirit recognizes its own powers as it puts its own faculties into operation and it is able to discover the

59. Presumably Evagrius refers here to faith as a psychic dynamism—such at least is suggested by the context. Among modern psychologists who treat this subject the best is Erik Erikson, *Identity and the Life Cycle* (New York, 1959), 55–65.

healing commandment through experiencing the impediments to its free movement.

83. The spirit that is engaged in the war against the passions does not see clearly the basic meaning of the war for it is something like a man fighting in the darkness of night. Once it has attained to purity of heart though, it distinctly makes out the designs of the enemy.

84. The goal of the ascetic life is charity; the goal of contemplative knowledge is theology. The beginnings of each are faith and contemplation of nature respectively. Such of the demons as fall upon the affective part of the soul are said to be the opponents of the ascetic life. Those again who disturb the rational part are the enemies of all truth and the adversaries of contemplation.

85. The drugs which purge the body do not remain within the body of the patient. The virtues, however, cleanse the soul but yet remain in the man who has been purified.

86. The rational soul operates according to nature when the following conditions are realized: the concupiscible part desires virtue; the irascible part fights to obtain it; the rational part, finally, applies itself to the contemplation of created things.

87. The man who is progressing in the ascetic life diminishes the force of passion. The man progressing in contemplation diminishes his ignorance. As regards the passions, the time will come when they will be entirely destroyed. In the matter of ignorance, however, one type will have an end, but another type will not.[60]

60. This passage is reminiscent of Gregory of Nyssa's teaching on *epektesis*, the doctrine that every arrival in the process of spiritual growth is but a new point of departure, and continued progress is the law of spiritual life even in the next world, in the beatific vision. See Jean Daniélou, *From Glory to Glory*, 56–71, and *Platonisme et Théologie Mystique* (Paris, 1944) for a more detailed discussion. E. Goutagny, ocso has supplied the translation for the last sentence in this difficult chapter.

88. Those things which are good or evil according as they are used well or ill are the objects making up virtue or vice. Prudence is the virtue that employs these objects for the one or the other.

89. According to our master, that man of wisdom, the rational soul is composed of three parts.[61] When virtue comes to birth in the rational part it is called prudence, understanding and wisdom. When it it developed in the concupiscible part it receives the names of temperance, charity and continence. Justice, however, is located in the whole of the soul. The virtue of the irascible part is termed courage and patience. Now the proper work of prudence is to war against the hostile powers and to protect the virtues, to draw up its forces against the vices, and to arrange affairs according to the requirements of the times. The province of understanding is to direct all those things which lead to our perfection in such a way that they harmoniously achieve their aim. Wisdom governs the contemplation of the meaningful structure of both corporeal and incorporeal objects.[62] Temperance has the function of enabling us to look upon those affairs which cause irrational phantasms, remaining the while free of passion. Charity has the role of showing itself to every image of God[63] as being as nearly like its prototype as possible no matter how the demons ply their arts to defile them. Continence has the power of refusing with joy every pleasure of the palate. The work of courage and patience is to know no fear of enemies and eagerly to endure afflictions. Finally, justice produces a certain harmony and symphony among the various parts of the soul.

90. The sheaves of grain are the fruit of seeds; the virtues have

61. Viller sees in this passage a reference to Gregory Nazianzen. Viller, *op. cit.*, 161, n. 13.

62. The "incorporeal objects" spoken of here are especially the angels considered in their providential role. This expression is found already in the Cappadocian Fathers (see Bouyer, *op. cit.*, 363), though it plays a much more important role in Evagrius' system.

63. "Every image of God" means every man no matter how little he may seem to reflect this image because of his vices.

knowledge as their fruit. As surely as tears go with the labor of sowing, joy attends the reaping.[64]

SAYINGS OF THE HOLY MONKS

91. It is a very necessary thing also to examine carefully the ways of the monks who have traveled, in an earlier age, straight along the road and to direct oneself along the same paths. Many excellent sayings and deeds are found that have been left behind by them. Among them is the following statement, told by one of their number. A dry and regular diet joined with charity leads the monk more quickly into the harbor of purity of heart. This same man delivered a certain brother from the disquieting specters by which he was visited in the night by ordering him to minister to the sick and to fast while he did it. When asked about his rationale for employing this procedure, he replied: "Such afflictions are extinguished by no other remedy so well as by mercy."

92. A certain member of what was then considered the circle of the wise once approached the just Anthony and asked him: "How do you ever manage to carry on, Father, deprived as you are of the consolation of books?" His reply: "My book, sir philosopher, is the nature of created things, and it is always at hand when I wish to read the words of God."[65]

93. The vessel of election, the elder Macarius the Egyptian, asked me: "Why is it that when we keep in mind the injuries that men do to us we destroy the faculty of memory in our souls, but when we remember that injury done us by the demons we keep it intact?" And when I found some difficulty in answering and went on to beg him to disclose the reason for this, he replied: "Because the first is against nature, whereas the second is in harmony with the nature of our souls."

64. Ps 125:6.
65. This saying is found in *Vitae Patrum*, 6, 4:16; PL 73:1018C.

94. I went over to see the holy Father Macarius at the very hottest time of day and since I was burning with thirst I asked him for a drink of water. He answered me: "Be content with the shade, for many there are who are making a journey on land or on sea who are deprived of this." Then as I struggled about temperance with him, wrestling with my thoughts, he told me: "Take courage, my son. For twenty full years I have not taken my fill of bread or water or sleep. I have eaten my bread by scant weight, and drunk my water by measure, and snatched a few winks of sleep while leaning against a wall."

95. The death of his father was announced to a certain monk. He turned to the messenger who had brought him the news and replied: "Stop your blasphemies. My father is immortal."[66]

96. One of the brethren asked of a certain old monk if he would advise him to eat with his mother and sisters when he went home. "Do not eat with women," was the answer of the old man.[67]

97. One of the brethren owned only a book of the Gospels. He sold this and gave the money for the support of the poor. He made a statement that deserves remembrance: "I have sold the very word that speaks to me saying: 'Sell your possessions and give to the poor.'"[68]

98. There is an island near Alexandria lying off the northern part of the lake that is called Maria. A monk of the most proved virtue lives there, a member of the colony of contemplatives. He states that all the actions of monks are performed through five causes: through God, through nature, through habit, through

---

66. We know from elsewhere this refers to Evagrius himself. LH, 38:13, p. 114.

67. Attributed to Abba Daniel, PG 65:153 (Daniel 2) and is anonymous in *Vitae Patrum,* 6, 4:19; PL 73:1018D.

68. *Vitae Patrum,* 5, 6:5; PL 73:889; also 3, 70; PL 73:772-73. These references are supplied by E. Goutagny who also points out that this saying is found in F. Nau, "Histoires des solitaires égyptiens," *Rev. de l'Orient Chrétien,* 13 (1908), 144, n. 392.

necessity, or through manual effort. The same monk again said that virtue is one by nature but that it is imitated variously by the powers of the soul. "For," he said, "the light of the sun is also without form but it is quite naturally given its form by the shape of the apertures through which it enters a room."[69]

99. On some other occasion another of the monks remarked as follows: "I have this reason for putting aside pleasure—that I might cut off the pretext for growing angry. For I know that anger constantly fights for pleasures and clouds the mind with passion that drives away contemplative knowledge."

There was another old monk who observed that "Charity does not know how to keep stores of food or money." It was this same old monk who stated that "I do not know that I have been deceived by the demons twice in the same matter."

100. It is not possible to love all the brethren to the same degree.[70] But it is possible to associate with all in a manner that is above passion, that is to say, free of resentment and hatred. One is to love the priests after the Lord, in as much as they purify us through the holy mysteries and pray for us. Our old men are to be honored like the angels for it is they who have anointed us for the battles and who treat the wounds we suffer from the bites of wild beasts.[71]

. . .

Let this suffice for now, my very dear Anatolius, for my discussion with you on the ascetic life. These are the gleanings that I have

69. This doctrine of the essential unity of the moral virtues was the Stoic teaching. Evagrius also speaks of it at the very beginning of his *Chapters on Prayer*. Cf. also M. Aubineau, "Traité de la Virginité," SC 119 (Paris, 1966), 448, n. 4.

70. This is an important statement for evaluating the real meaning of Evagrius' teaching on the perfectibility of human nature. It is rather in his speculations than in his observations that he is too absolute and extreme.

71. That is to say by the oil of their discretion and empathetic insight.

gathered, by the grace of the Holy Spirit, among the growths of our ripening vine. But if the bright "sun of justice" will shine upon us and our cluster becomes ripe then we shall also drink its wine "which rejoices the heart of man,"[72] through the prayers and intercession of the just Gregory[73] who planted me as well as those of the holy Fathers of the present time who water me, and also by the power of Jesus Christ our Lord who makes me grow. May praise and power be his for ages without end. Amen.

72. Ps 103:15.

73. St Gregory Nazianzen is the one referred to here. This context suggests that Gregory had recently died. Cf. TP 715.

CHAPTERS ON PRAYER

INTRODUCTION

THE THEOLOGICAL ACHIEVEMENT that is represented by this short treatise is doubtless the most durable of Evagrius' productions. Its important place in the history of spirituality has already been noted above.[1]

What is the precise nature of Evagrius' contribution to the theology of prayer, and to its practice?

The central focus of this doctrine is found in those several chapters which stress the relationship between prayer and contemplation. In particular, it is the identification between the highest summits of contemplation and the purest form of prayer that is the heart of the Evagrian theology of prayer.[2] A more careful analysis of other related passages in this and other works of the author reveals that this identification extends to each of the stages of the spiritual life; progress in contemplation means progress in prayer; progress in prayer means progress in contemplation.[3]

In some sense Evagrius chooses to identify prayer and contemplation with the monastic life—even with the spiritual life itself.

The implications of this teaching are better seen, perhaps, when one compares the relatively small place given to contemplation by even some of the greatest monastic legislators, such as St Basil, or Theodore Studite.[4] St Benedict, without excluding the activity of

---

1. See p. xcii. 2. Hausherr, *Leçons*, 80–82. 3. *Ibid.*

4. St Theodore Studite was an eighth century monk who gave the influential "Typikon" (monastic rule) to the monastery of Studios in Constantinople. This Typikon was marked by a concern for those same values of communal

contemplation in any way, does not use the word or any equivalent in his *Rule,* although he clearly expects his monks to turn to Cassian where they will find this doctrine stated. Humility, obedience, the works of charity—all these would be presented as norms for determining spiritual progress by these men. Such norms, of course, give a determining spirit to the monasteries that accept them. To the extent that a monastery or a monastic tradition accepts these norms for progress rather than the norm given by Evagrius, they will possess a different spirit than the one he sought to inculcate. It is quite conceivable that a Benedictine monk, having climbed the degrees of humility, would achieve the heights of perfection without giving much place to contemplation in his life. The same holds true for a monk in St Basil's community who would have devoted himself to obedience and the service of the sick. But for one trained in the Evagrian spirituality, prayer—is—contemplation, such a thing is not possible. The monk may have achieved a form and measure of perfection, but it would not correspond to Evagrius' ideal.[5]

In some sense all else flows from this principle. There is, for instance, the great intensity of purpose with which Evagrius places prayer above all else as a state to be achieved and maintained. The ardor and intensity that everywhere abound in his writings find a

---

life that characterize the Rules of St Basil. In particular it gives considerable prominence to the liturgy as an observance of monks leading to their sanctification. His spirituality has proved deeply influential for wide segments of the Byzantine monastic world. J. LeRoy, "La Réforme Studite," *Il Monachismo Orientale* (Rome, 1958), 118–124, for a good study of the Typikon. Studite spirituality stands in a state of tension with the Hesychastic form that is more individualistic. L. Bouyer, "La Spiritualité Byzantine," *Histoire de la Spiritualité Chrétienne,* L. Bouyer, F. Vandenbroucke, J. Leclercq (Paris, 1961), 648–96. That the monasticism of Theodore and of St Basil is not devoid of the contemplative spirit has been shown by S. Rendina, *La contemplazione negli scritti di S. Basilio Magno* (Rome, 1959).

5. Evagrius himself is very explicit on this point. "The effects of keeping the commandments (i.e. *apatheia*) do not suffice to heal the powers of the soul completely. They must be complemented by a contemplative activity appropriate to these faculties and this activity must penetrate the spirit." *Praktikos,* 79.

focal point here, and lend a characteristic note to his doctrine on prayer. "Prayer is the most divine of the virtues."[6] Again, "by its very nature the spirit is made to pray."[7]

Evagrius, we have said, tends to equate the whole of Christian life with the life of prayer. The way he employs a familiar Scripture text demonstrates this quite convincingly. "Go, sell your possessions and give to the poor, and take up your cross so that you can pray without distraction."[8] Instead of this last clause the Gospel text reads here, "and come follow me."[9] Thus, for our author, to pray without distraction equals to follow Christ. A bold transposition which no reader could miss who was familiar with the Gospels.

So true is it that prayer is the following of Christ that no man can be saved without it. Yet it surpasses the powers of man to achieve, so that it must be received as a gift from God.[10] It is the greatest of his gifts; nothing more precious is to be found on earth. "What greater thing is there than to converse intimately with God and to be preoccupied with his company?"[11]

It is well known that the ideal for the early Church in the period prior to Constantine was martyrdom. It was considered such a great thing by some because it was a more perfect imitation of Christ, who died for the sake of sinners. In any case, it was viewed as a signal victory of Christ over the Devil, renewed in the person of his faithful witness. When peace was restored to the Church this ideal shifted to that of witnessing to Christ through the life of virginity, asceticism and prayer—the monastic life.

The theology of martyrdom took on a new character with the teaching of Origen. He had taught that martyrdom was the sign of perfection because it was the best way to show that the Christian aspired to the contemplative knowledge of God.[12] In other words, he claims a value for martyrdom in terms of its relationship to a higher good, namely contemplation.

---

6. *Chapters on Prayer*, 150.
7. *Praktikos*, 49. See also *Chapters on Prayer*, 65.   8. *Chapters on Prayer*, 17.
9. Mt. 19:21.   10. *Chapters on Prayer*, 58, 62, 69.   11. *Ibid.*, 34.
12. Origen, *Prayer, Exhortation to Martyrdom*, trans. J. O'Meara, ACW, 19 (1954), 186.

Evagrius, in this as in so many other points of doctrine, took the teaching of Origen a step further. *He makes contemplation the equivalent of martyrdom.* There is a whole series of chapters in the present treatise which give a basis for asserting this.[13] (Remember that ardent prayer is contemplation.) He tells us of men who suffered the most astonishing torments from demons, sustaining them willingly rather than renounce—not Christ, indeed, but prayer. Above all he speaks with the most obvious admiration of a "certain spiritual man about whom we have read. While he was praying one day a viper crawled up to him and seized his foot. He did not so much as lower his arms until he finished his customary prayer, and he suffered no harm whatever from thus loving God above his own self."[14]

More than this, prayer lifts man above his very nature, to set him on a level with the angels. "By true prayer a monk becomes the equal of an angel."[15] By his contemplation he also becomes a temple of God.[16] Finally, it elevates him to the knowledge of the very Trinity itself.[17] Indeed, in attaining to this gift of prayer a man becomes "heir to all things."[18] Then only is he fully himself for "by its very nature the spirit is made to pray."[19]

Another important feature of Evagrian doctrine on prayer is the stress that he places on its *purity.* By this *purity* he means it is beyond all limiting concepts, beyond any idea, however noble or lofty or elevated, that stands between the soul and the Trinity, who is not only beyond all forms but is beyond multiplicity. The Trinity is Simplicity, and thus can be approached only in the greatest simplicity of spirit. In this theology, all clear distinct ideas are a form of ignorance; true knowledge is an infinite ignorance.[20] The passages where he refers to immateriality[21] and formlessness at the

---

13. *Chapters on Prayer,* 106–111, esp. 109.

14. *Ibid.,* 109.   15. *Ibid.,* 113.   16. *Kephalaia Gnostica,* 5:84.

17. *Ibid.,* 2:47; 3:12.   18. *Chapters on Prayer,* 36.   19. *Praktikos,* 49.

20. *Kephalaia Gnostica,* 3:88. See also I. Hausherr, "Ignorance infinie ou science infinie?" OCP 25 (1959), 44–52, and again *Leçons,* 150f.

21. *Chapters on Prayer,* 66, and also 70 where he states that "Prayer is the rejection of concepts."

time of prayer[22] are express statements of this noesis of mystic union.

Many of these chapters deal with some one or other of the emotions, or passions as Evagrius usually calls them. How this fits into his theology of prayer is not the least interesting of points for discussion. For Evagrius is a consummate psychologist. His knowledge of dynamic psychology is remarkable indeed, but still more interesting is his awareness of its significance for the life of prayer.

For Evagrius it is unthinkable that a man should aspire to be united with God in pure prayer without first cleansing his heart fully. Only when he has attained *apatheia,* a state of abiding calm deriving from full harmony of the passions, can he speak of perfect charity. Only when he has perfect charity can he hope to know God.[23] This same doctrine is presupposed in this work on prayer. Thus, the man who would attain to perfect prayer must always be alert to guard against losing purity of heart. To properly guard against this loss he must have a knowledge of the chief *logismoi,* that is to say, passionate thoughts. He must also have an intimate knowledge of the demons who tempt us through these thoughts.[24]

Because prayer is the source of union with the Trinity, the fount of all true joy, Evagrius invites us to forsake all lesser things and to seek our all from a life dedicated to prayer. Prayer itself becomes our joy.[25] So much so that true prayer can be found only where joy is found, in nothing less than God himself.[26] Prayer itself is the fruit of the thanksgiving and joy that derive from the living knowledge of God.[27]

Few voices have sung the praises of contemplative prayer more ardently than the monk of Nitria. "Pray always" and "watch and pray" were, quite literally, watchwords of the early Church. In reading these chapters on prayer by Evagrius we listen to the voice of this same Church as it rang out the changes on the great theme of

---

22. *Ibid.,* 117, 120.
23. *The Epistle to Anatolius,* above, p. 14; also *Kephalaia Gnostica,* 1:86.';
24. *Praktikos,* 34.   25. *Chapters on Prayer,* 16.   26. *Ibid.,* 153.
27. *Ibid.,* 15.

prayer. "Pray always," she seems to tell us through him, "for in prayer you become fully a man, and learn your own dignity.[28] But above all in prayer you will go on increasing in your love for God,[29] until the day when, in eternity, vision obtains what you once sought in prayer."

The Text

The textual version followed in this translation is that found in Migne *Patrologia Graeca,* volume seventy-nine, among the works of St Nilus of Sinai. No critical edition has been published to date. It has been possible, however, to make some few corrections by reference to the Coislin ms 109. This is cited in the very valuable notes of Hausherr's work.[30] The Greek text of the *Philokalia* which also contains this treatise under the name of St Nilus[31] has also been used for some readings.

As regards the translation itself, the Latin version published in Migne has often been useful, but, quite often too, inadequate. Hausherr's masterful translation, with its erudite notes, has been unfailingly helpful in making the sense come through while remaining faithful to a very concise and technical idiom that characterizes Evagrius' Greek style.

Date and Dedication

One last question remains—the date of composition and the person to whom the work is sent. From Evagrius' opening remarks it is likely that he wrote it in the last years of his life. Palladius tells us that he was ill with stomach trouble during these last years,[32] and

28. *Ibid.,* 84.   29. *Ibid.,* 118.
30. *Les Leçons d'un Contemplative* (Paris, 1960).
31. In the *Philokalia* it is printed in vol. 1, 176–189.
32. LH, 38:13, P. 114.

Evagrius mentions at the end of his dedicatory letter that he is ill. Further, the content of this work reveals that the author is in full possession of his developed thought, and that he has a broad and long experience of the life of prayer and asceticism though he has not yet achieved *apatheia*. The date of composition then was probably between 390 and 395.

To whom does he send this treatise? There are only a few suggestions in the dedicatory epistle. First of all, it seems to have been someone who had been an Egyptian hermit, at least for a time, and who had Marcarius the Great for a teacher just as Evagrius himself did. Clearly too he is a man of some learning and intelligence, familiar with Hellenistic speculations on numbers. From the familiar tone of the letter he must have lived for a considerable time as a friend of Evagrius and in his immediate company. On the other hand, he considers Evagrius as superior to him and even as his master in some respects. Lastly, there is the fact that he was, at the time of Evagrius' illness, living some distance away and had been doing so for an extended period. Finally, it is clear that Evagrius wrote in response to a repeated request.

We know that Evagrius and Rufinus maintained a correspondence throughout the years that Rufinus continued to live on Mt Olivet in his monastery and that Evagrius lived in Egypt. Since Rufinus also had spent time in Egypt, and since he and Evagrius maintained the friendliest of relations till death separated them, he fits the facts better than anyone else we know. While it remains uncertain that he is the one whose request prompted the composition of this work which was to have such a profound effect upon the spirituality of the Christian world, yet it is an intriguing possibility that Rufinus is the friend for whom this work was compiled by the author.

THE 153 CHAPTERS ON PRAYER

IT WAS SO CHARACTERISTIC of you[1] to get a letter to me just at a time when I was aflame with the hot urgings of my own impure passions and my spirit was afflicted with all kinds of vile thoughts. This kindness of yours was a true consolation to me. By it you prove to be, fortunately, a worthy pupil of our great leader and teacher.[2] I must say, however, that I find it hardly surprising that your efforts bear such fruit, for you have always been favored with the most conspicuous good fortune. In fact, you put me in mind of that God-favored man Jacob. You know his story well—how he so courageously bowed his back to labor seven long years so as to obtain the hand of Rachel, and then, through some deception, received Leah instead.[3] Well, as he then went on to ask for her who was his heart's desire—though he had to work another seven years to obtain her—you too go on to ask for your heart's desire.[4]

As for myself, I would not deny that I have worked the whole

---

1. Perhaps it is Rufinus who is addressed here. This seems the more likely addressee, although there is no certain proof.

2. *Fortunately:* in Greek the word is μακαρίως, an obvious pun on the name of Evagrius' great teacher, Macarius.

3. Gen. 29:15–30.

4. Apparently Evagrius had an earlier request from his friend to compose such a work as he now sends to him, and had neglected to comply. The Greek here is highly condensed, even to the point of being elliptical. Our translation renders it in an expanded form to bring out the meaning more clearly.

night through and have caught nothing.[5] But, nonetheless, at your command I went ahead and cast my net and have come up with a whole netful of fish. Not big ones, to be sure, but still a goodly number—one hundred and fifty-three all told.[6] I send them on to you in the basket of charity, in the form of these hundred and fifty-three chapters. So then, this is my way of carrying out your orders to me.

Now let me express my admiration of you and the strong sense of envy I experience over that excellent purpose of yours which leads you to desire so earnestly these chapters on prayer. It is not merely these characters written on parchment with ink that you love, but also those which are firmly planted in the spirit[7] by charity and by the absence of all resentment.[8]

Now since "everything exists in pairs, one set over against the other," as Ben Sirach, that man of wisdom, says,[9] receive this gift in both its dimensions, that is to say, as a piece of writing and as a vehicle of the spirit. You realize, of course, that the spirit has precedence over the letter, for without the spirit there could be no such thing as letters. So also in the case of prayer there is a two-fold division, one the active, the other the contemplative type. Then too the same situation prevails in the field of mathematics where we have one kind of number more concrete and indicating quantity, but also the element of positive and negative, the qualitative factor.[10]

5. Lk. 5:5.   6. Jn. 21:11.

7. 2 Cor. 3:3. The word translated by *spirit* here is νοῦς. It is not without significance that whereas St Paul had employed the word heart (καρδία), Evagrius changes it to express his intellectualist emphasis, and his bias toward contemplation, which is the proper activity of the νοῦς. For Evagrius man is not, essentially, a creature composed of body and soul, but a νοῦς, that is, an intelligence whose proper activity is religious contemplation.

8. ἀμνησικακία. This virtue was to have a long history and play an important part in Byzantine spirituality. Literally it means the forgetting of injuries. Evagrius feels this virtue is essential to the calm necessary for contemplative prayer.

9. Sir, 42:24.

10. The symbolism of numbers held a place of honor in antiquity. Whereas a good deal of the effort to find symbolic meanings hidden under various numbers seems altogether arbitrary to us, the ancients, from the times at least

Well then we have divided this treatise on prayer into one hundred and fifty-three chapters and now send on to you this dish that is flavored by the Gospels[11] in the hope that you might discover in it the relish of a symbolic number that contains the form of both a triangle and a hexagon. For these figures represent the devout knowledge of the Trinity and the circumscription of this ordered cosmos respectively. Whereas the number one hundred is, by itself, a square, the number fifty-three is both triangular and spherical. How so? Well, fifty-three is made up of the sum of twenty-five and twenty-eight. The number twenty-eight is triangular of itself; the number twenty-five is spherical for it contains the product of five times five. And so in this number you have a square figure to express the fourfold number of the virtues, but also the spherical which, because of its form, represents the circular movements of time and is an apt symbol for deep knowledge of

---

of Pythagoras, had much confidence in its validity. Our own times are recovering some of this confidence. Sir James Jeans has said that when God created the universe he thought as a mathematician.

11. This flavor of the Gospels comes from the 153 fish, whose number determines the number of chapters in this treatise. In other words Evagrius intends his work to be read along with, not as a substitute for the Gospels. This very probably explains certain omissions otherwise surprising, such as references to sacraments, to the person of Jesus, and the like.

Perhaps it was St Jerome who provided the right solution to the meaning of the 153 fish of great size when he observed that, according to the opinion of Oppianus of Cilicia, there are 153 species of fish (PL 25:474). Thus the passage—assuming with Lagrange that this view was a wide-spread one in antiquity, and known to the Evangelist—refers symbolically to the universality of the Church. This means that the catch has a deeper theological meaning than just a manifestation of the miraculous power of the Risen Christ. That Oppianus does not seem to say this in so many words is not too important for our purposes; the important thing is that it was a widely accepted belief, the experts' view, in early Christian times. M. J. Lagrange, *Evangile selon Saint Jean* (Paris, 1948), 526f.

Regarding the technical discussion in the rest of this paragraph, the special significance of a triangle, square, hexagon and a spherical number, the best discussion is that found in the notes to the Dutch translation of this work; "Opgang van de Geest naar God," trans. Christoforo Wagenaar ocso, *Tijdschrift voor Geestelijk Leven* (1969), 444–46. It was especially the Pythagoreans who gave a certain scientific form to the symbolism of numbers.

this world. For in the revolutions of time week follows upon week, month upon month, year turns upon year and season upon season, as we observe by the movements of the sun and moon, of the spring and summer and the like.

Now the triangle, on the other hand, represented, as we have said already, by the number twenty-eight, symbolizes the knowledge of the Blessed Trinity. Or else one might consider the figure one hundred and fifty-three triangular by virtue of the sum of its component numbers and then it would stand for the ascetical life, the contemplation of nature and theology;[12] or it might represent faith, hope and charity; or again, gold, silver and precious stones.

Let these remarks suffice then for our discussion concerning the meaning of numbers. As regards these chapters themselves, do not make fun of their insignificant appearance. You are a man who has learned to be content with much or little. Besides I am sure you remember the One who did not disdain the two cents that the widow gave as an offering; how he received them in preference to the rich gifts of many others. Since you have the gift of preserving the fruit of kindness and charity for your true brothers, pray for a sick man that he may recover his health, pick up his mat and henceforth walk about freely by the grace of Christ. Amen.[13]

THE CHAPTERS

1. If a man wishes to prepare a fragrant perfume he must make a mixture of pure incense, of cinnamon, of onyx-stone and of myrrh in equal parts as the law prescribes.[14] This mixture is the fourfold number of the virtues.[15] If they are found in full strength and in due proportions then the spirit will not be betrayed.

---

12. πρακτική, φυσική, θεολογική, These are the three elements comprising the mystery of Christ. *Praktikos*, 1.

13. Mk. 2:11.   14. Ex. 30:34.

15. The essential unity of the moral virtues, originally a Stoic doctrine, was taught to Evagrius by Gregory Nazianzen. See Hausherr, *Leçons*, 14, and the note there. Also see above, note 69 p. 41.

2. The soul that is purified by the plenitude of virtues renders the spirit unshakable in its balance and makes it capable of possessing the state for which it longs.[16]

3. Prayer is a continual intercourse of the spirit with God. What state of soul then is required that the spirit might thus strain after its Master without wavering, living constantly with him without intermediary?[17]

4. If Moses, when he attempted to draw near the burning bush, was prohibited until he should remove the shoes from his feet,[18] how should you not free yourself of every thought that is colored by passion seeing that you wish to see One who is beyond every thought and perception?

5. Pray first for the gift of tears so that by means of sorrow you may soften your native rudeness.[19] Then having confessed your sins to the Lord you will obtain pardon for them.

6. Pray with tears and your request will find a hearing. Nothing so gratifies the Lord as supplication offered in the midst of tears.

7. Though fountains of tears flow during your prayer do not begin to consider yourself better than others. For your prayers have merely obtained the help you need to confess your sins with readiness and to conciliate the favor of the Lord.

---

16. The state it longs for is, of course, the state of pure prayer, of contemplation of the Blessed Trinity, or theology. On the significance of the word κατάστασις see above, note 51, p. 32.

17. This translation follows the text of the *Philokalia*, where ἰσχύσῃ stands in place of ἡσυχάσῃ of the Migne version and ἐκταθῆναι for ἐκσταθῆναι. See *Leçons*, 16, note 30, where Hausherr points out these as correct readings.

18. Ex. 3:5.

19. This passage is reminiscent of an expression used by St John of the Cross in *The Flame of Divine Love: rudeza natural*. Evagrius uses the word ἀγριότης. See *Leçons*, 19, where Hausherr discusses this point.

8. So then do not turn the very antidote of passion into passion[20] if you do not wish to offer further provocation to One who has given you this grace. This madness has led any number of persons astray. They have lost sight of the purpose of their tears even while weeping for their sins.

9. Stand resolute, fully intent on your prayer. Pay no heed to the concerns and thoughts that might arise the while. They do nothing better than disturb and upset you so as to dissolve the fixity of your purpose.

10. When the devils see that you are really fervent in your prayer they suggest certain matters to your mind, giving you the impression that there are pressing concerns demanding attention. In a little while they stir up your memory of these matters and move your mind to search into them. Then when it meets with failure it becomes saddened and loses heart.

11. Strive to render your mind deaf and dumb at the time of prayer and then you will be able to pray.

12. When you find yourself tempted or contradicted; or when you get irritated or when you grow angry through encountering some opposition or feel the urge to utter some kind of invective— then is the time to put yourself in mind of prayer and of the judgment to be passed on such doings. You will find that the disordered movement will immediately be stilled.

13. Whatever you might do by way of avenging yourself on a brother who has done you some injustice will turn into a stumbling block for you at the time of prayer.

14. Prayer is the fair flower of meekness and mildness.

20. That is to say, do not yield to vainglory over possessing the gift of tears, for if you do, you destroy what you build up.

15. Prayer is the fruit of joy and of thanksgiving.

16. Prayer is the exclusion of sadness and despondency.

17. Go, sell your possessions and give to the poor, and take up your cross so that you can pray without distraction.

18. If you wish to pray worthily, deny yourself every hour. Playing the part of a wise man, study and work very hard to learn to endure much for the sake of prayer.

19. Whatever difficulty you patiently endure through love of wisdom will reap ripe fruits at the time of prayer.

20. If you desire to pray as you ought do not sadden anyone. Otherwise you run in vain.[21]

21. "Leave your gift before the altar and go be reconciled with your brother,"[22] our Lord said—and then you shall pray undisturbed. For resentment blinds the reason of the man who prays and casts a cloud over his prayer.

22. The man who stores up injuries and resentments and yet fancies that he prays might as well draw water from a well and pour it into a cask that is full of holes.

23. If you know how to practice patience you shall ever pray with joy.

24. When you are praying such matters will come to mind as would seem clearly to justify your getting angry. But anger is

21. The thought of the injured brother will return at times of prayer and prevent you from drawing near to God in peace and with a pure conscience. This idea is stressed elsewhere by Evagrius, in various forms: *Chapters on Prayer*, 24, 25, 26, 27, 45, 53, etc.

22. Mt. 5:24.

completely unjustified against your neighbor. If you really try you will find some way to arrange the matter without showing anger. So then, employ every device to avoid a display of anger.

25. Beware lest while appearing to heal another you do something to make yourself incurable and thus do serious damage to your prayer.

26. If you restrain your anger you yourself will be spared and in the process prove yourself too wise a man to indulge in arrogance. Further you will be counted among the men of prayer.

27. Armed as you are against anger do not submit to any powerful desire. For it is these which provide fuel for anger, and anger in turn is calculated to cloud the eye of your spirit and destroy your state of prayer.

28. Do not pray by outward gestures only, but bend your mind as well to the perception of spiritual prayer with great fear.

29. At times just as soon as you rise to pray you pray well.[23] At other times, work as you may, you achieve nothing. But this happens so that by seeking still more intently, and then finally reaching the mark, you may possess your prize without fear of loss.

30. When an angel makes his presence felt by us, all disturbing thoughts immediately disappear. The spirit finds itself clothed in great tranquility. It prays purely. At other times, though, we are beset with the customary struggle and then the spirit joins the fight. It cannot so much as raise its eyes for it is overtaken by diverse passions. Yet if only the spirit goes on striving it will achieve its purpose. When it knocks on the door hard enough it will be opened.

23. The Migne edition has οὐ instead of εὖ and so reads "you do not pray." But Hausherr's emendation seems valid. The Latin translation has made the same correction.

31. Pray not to this end, that your own desires be fulfilled. You can be sure they do not fully accord with the will of God. Once you have learned to accept this point, pray instead that "thy will be done" in me. In every matter ask him in this way for what is good and for what confers profit on your soul, for you yourself do not seek this so completely as he does.

32. Many times while I was at prayer, I would keep asking for what seemed good to me. I kept insisting on my own request, unreasonably putting pressure on the will of God. I simply would not leave it up to his Providence to arrange what he knew would turn out for my profit. Finally, when I obtained my request I became greatly chagrined at having been so stubborn about getting my own way, for in the end the matter did not turn out to be what I had fancied it would.

33. What else is there that is good besides God alone? Therefore let us cast all our concerns upon him and it will be well with us. Certainly, he who is wholly good is necessarily the kind of person who gives only good gifts.

34. Do not be over-anxious and strain yourself so as to gain an immediate hearing for your request. The Lord wishes to confer greater favors than those you ask for, in reward for your perseverance in praying to him. For what greater thing is there than to converse intimately with God and to be preoccupied with his company?[24] Undistracted prayer is the highest act of the intellect.[25]

35. Prayer is an ascent of the spirit to God.

---

24. This translation follows the *Philokalia* rather than Migne. Modern scriptural exegesis provides an interesting parallel to this thought of Evagrius when Ruldolph Bultmann, in his exegesis of 1 Jn. 5:15, remarks that "prayer itself is already its own answer," in R. Bultmann, *Theology of the New Testament*, trans. K. Grobel, vol. 2 (London, 1955), 87.

25. The Migne edition omits this last sentence. It is found as no. 35 in the *Philokalia*.

36. Do you long to pray? Renounce all things. You then will become heir to all.

37. First of all pray to be purified from your passions. Secondly, pray to be delivered from ignorance. Thirdly, pray to be freed from all temptation and abandonment.

38. In your prayer seek only after justice and the kingdom of God, that is to say, after virtue and true spiritual knowledge. Then all else will be given to you besides.

39. It is a part of justice that you should pray not only for your own purification but also for that of every man. In doing this you will imitate the practice of the angels.[26]

40. Observe whether you truly stand before God in your prayer or whether you are under some compulsion that drives you to seek recognition from men, striving in this manner after their approval. When indulged to this end your protracted prayer is nothing better than a pretext.[27]

41. Whether you pray along with the brethren or alone, strive to make your prayer more than a mere habit. Make it a true inner experience.

42. The specific quality of prayer is that it is a respectful gravity which is colored by compunction. It has something of a deepfelt sorrow about it, the kind one feels when, amid silent groans, he really admits his sins.

43. If your spirit still looks around at the time of prayer, then it

26. As this chapter reveals, the angelic life for Evagrius does not only mean a life of elevated contemplation (c. 113, below), but also the practice of a superior form of selfless love for others.

27. As Hausherr suggests, we follow here the reading of the *Philokalia* which has παρατάσει instead of παραστάσει.

does not yet pray as a monk. You are no better than a man of affairs engaged in a kind of landscape gardening.[28]

44. When you pray keep your memory under close custody. Do not let it suggest your own fancies to you, but rather have it convey the awareness of your reaching out to God. Remember this—the memory has a powerful proclivity for causing detriment to the spirit at the time of prayer.

45. When you are at prayer the memory activates fantasies of either past happenings or of fresh concerns or else of persons you have previously injured.

46. The devil so passionately envies the man who prays that he employs every device to frustrate that purpose. Thus he does not cease to stir up thoughts of various affairs by means of the memory. He stirs up all the passions by means of the flesh. In this way he hopes to offer some obstacle to that excellent course pursued in prayer on the journey toward God.

47. When the depraved demon has done all he can and still finds that his efforts to prevent the prayer of the virtuous man are unavailing, he will let up for a time. But again after a while he avenges himself on this man of prayer. For he will either enkindle the man's anger and thus dissipate that excellent state established in him by prayer, or else he chooses to outrage the spirit by provoking it to some unreasonable pleasure.

48. When you have prayed well expect some untoward happenings and stand manfully ready to defend your gains. For from the beginning you were made for this: to work and to watch. And so when you have wrought some work do not let it go unguarded. If you fail to act in this way you shall profit nothing from your prayer.

---

28. For Evagrius the monk is more a spirit (νοῦς) than a mere man; he lives on a plane where the light of the Blessed Trinity is more real than the light of the sun. See *Leçons*, 64–66, for Hausherr's penetrating comments.

49. Every war fought between us and the impure spirits is engaged in for no other cause than that of spiritual prayer. This is an activity that is intolerable to them, they find it so hostile and oppressive. To us, on the other hand, it is both pleasant in the highest degree and spiritually profitable.

50. Why do the demons wish to commit acts of gluttony, impurity, avarice, wrath, resentment and the other evil passions in us? Here is the reason—that the spirit in this way should become dull and consequently rendered unfit to pray. For when man's irrational passions are thriving he is not free to pray and to seek the word of God.

51. We seek after virtues for the sake of attaining to the inner meaning of created things. We pursue these latter, that is to say the inner meanings of what is created, for the sake of attaining to the Lord who has created them. It is in the state of prayer that he is accustomed to manifest himself.

52. The state of prayer can be aptly described as a habitual state of imperturbable calm (ἀπάθεια). It snatches to the heights of intelligible reality the spirit which loves wisdom and which is truly spiritualized by the most intense love.

53. The man who strives after true prayer must learn to master not only anger and his lust, but must free himself from every thought that is colored by passion.

54. The man who loves God constantly lives and speaks with him as a Father. He turns aside from every thought that is tinged with passion.

55. One who has become free of disturbing passion does not necessarily truly pray. It is quite possible for a man to have none but the purest thoughts and yet be so distracted mulling over them that he remains the while far removed from God.

56. Even when the spirit does avoid getting involved with these simple thoughts of things,[29] it does not by that fact alone attain to the place of prayer.[30] It may get involved in the contemplation of objects and waste time in considering their inner nature. For even though these concepts be simple, considerations of real things that they are, they do impress a certain form on the spirit and draw one far away from God.

57. Even if the spirit should rise above the contemplation of corporeal nature, still it does not as yet see the perfect place of God. For it might well be engaged in the contemplation of intelligible things and partake of their multiplicity.

58. If you wish to pray then it is God whom you need. He it is who gives prayer to the man who prays. On that account call upon him saying: "Hallowed be thy Name, thy Kingdom come," that is, the Holy Spirit and your Only-Begotten Son. This is what our Lord taught us when he said: "The Father is adored in Spirit and in Truth."[31]

59. A man who worships in Spirit and Truth no longer honors the Creator because of his works, but praises him because of himself.

29. This penetration to "simple" thoughts, that is to say, those free of disturbing and excessive passion, is a key step in the Evagrian ascent to God. *Chapters on Prayer*, 66, 68–70, etc. This term ψίλος, simple, understood in this acceptation would have a long history in Byzantine and also in Western theology. Eckhart, for instance, gives it considerable importance. See Sullivan *op. cit.*, 291. Hausherr points out that this c. 56, with the one preceding it, the one following it, and c. 60, are the heart of Evagrian teaching on prayer; *Leçons*, 80.

30. The *place of prayer* (προσευχῆς τόπος) is another of Evagrius' technical terms. It is derived from the term *place of God* (τόπος θεοῦ), which refers to the experience of God's presence. It is based on the Septuagint account of the appearance of God to Moses and the elders on Sinai. Ex. 24:10–11.

31. Jn. 4:24. This translation follows the text of the *Philokalia*. The Migne edition adds a phrase at the end: τὸν θεόν, τουτέστι τὸν Πατέρα, ἐπεὶ καὶ τὰ τρία θεός. (See *Leçons*, 82, note 12, where Hausherr points out that it is a gloss.)

60. If you are a theologian you truly pray. If you truly pray you are a theologian.[32]

61. When your spirit withdraws, as it were, little by little from the flesh because of your ardent longing for God, and turns away from every thought that derives from sensibility or memory[33] or temperament and is filled with reverence and joy at the same time, then you can be sure that you are drawing near that country whose name is prayer.

62. The Holy Spirit takes compassion on our weakness, and though we are impure he often comes to visit us. If he should find our spirit praying to him out of love for the truth he then descends upon it and dispels the whole army of thoughts and reasonings that beset it. And too he urges it on to the works[34] of spiritual prayer.

63. Whereas others derive their reasonings and ideas and principles from the changing states of the body, yet God does the contrary. He descends upon the spirit itself and infuses his knowledge into it as he pleases. Calm peace he brings to the body's disturbed state through the spirit.

64. No one who loves true prayer and yet gives way to anger or resentment can be absolved from the imputation of madness. For he resembles a man who wishes to see clearly and for this purpose he scratches his eyes.

65. If you long to pray then avoid all that is opposed to prayer. Then when God draws near he has only to go along with you.

32. This chapter is one of the key passages for the full understanding of the Evagrian identification of contemplation with prayer. See Hausherr, *Leçons*, 85 f.

33. *Memory*: this word is added from the *Philokalia*; it is lacking in Migne.

34. A variant reading has ἔρωτα, not ἔργα. This would be translated "love of spiritual prayer." See Hausherr, *Leçons*, 88.

66. When you are praying do not fancy the Divinity like some image formed within yourself. Avoid also allowing your spirit to be impressed with the seal of some particular shape, but rather, free from all matter, draw near the immaterial Being and you will attain to understanding.

67. Beware of the traps your adversaries lay for you. For suddenly it may happen when you are praying purely, free from all disturbance, that some unusual and strange form appears so as to lead you into the presumptuous thought that God is actually situated there as in a place. This is calculated to persuade you, through the very suddenness of the revelation, that God is something quantitative. But God is without quantity and without all outward form.

68. When the destructive demon is unable to stir up your memory at the time of prayer, then he does some violence to the bodily equilibrium so as to cause a certain strange phantasm to rise in the spirit and to assume a particular shape there. Then the man who is accustomed to stop short at concepts is readily brought low. In this manner then the spirit, which by its nature is driven ahead in its search for immaterial knowledge and for that which is beyond all form, goes astray. It mistakes the smoke for the light.

69. Stand guard over your spirit, keeping it free of concepts at the time of prayer so that it may remain in its own deep calm. Thus he who has compassion on the ignorant will come to visit even such an insignificant person as yourself. That is when you will receive the most glorious gift of prayer.

70. You will not be able to pray purely if you are all involved with material affairs and agitated with unremitting concerns. For prayer is the rejection of concepts.

71. A man in chains cannot run. Nor can the mind that is enslaved to passion see the place of spiritual prayer. It is dragged

along and tossed by these passion-filled thoughts and cannot stand firm and tranquil.

72. When the spirit prays purely without being led astray then the demons no longer come upon it from the left side but from the right. That is to say, they suggest the semblance of God to it in the form of some image that is flattering to the senses, in the hope of leading it to think it has attained the aim of its prayer. Now a certain contemplative man—an excellent person—has remarked that this phenomenon is due to the passion of vainglory and also to the influence of a demon who stimulates a specific site of the brain and thus agitates the cerebral circulation.[35]

73. I hold to the view that this demon whom I have just spoken of plays a light upon the spirit as he wills. This is his way of stirring up the passion of vainglory. He thus produces a train of reasoning that leads the spirit, all unawares,[36] to give a form to the divine and essential knowledge. Then such a one comes to believe that no hostile force is at work in him, aware as he is that there are no impure disturbances of his flesh, and that, on the contrary he experiences only purity. So he draws the conclusion that the apparition is divine in origin. But in truth it is produced in him by the demon, who, as I have said, makes use of this frightful tactic of stimulating this site of the brain and provoking some change in the light phenomenon controlled by it, thereby causing the above-described change in the spirit.

74. When the angel of the Lord visits us he dispels by his word alone every conflicting force acting in us, and brings it about that the light of our spirit operates without deception.

35. This chapter is very interesting for the awareness it reveals of the relation between the emotions and the physiology of the brain. Only in very recent times have the details of this relation been worked out in considerable detail through the discovery and description of the Limbic pathways.

36. κουφογνώμων a very rare word in Greek. See Hausherr's note in *Leçons*, 107, note 10.

L

75. The statement in the Apocalypse that speaks of the angel who takes care of putting incense in the bowl that contains the prayer of the saints refers, in my opinion, to precisely this grace wrought by the angel. He infuses knowledge of true prayer so that for the future the spirit may stand firm, free of all *acedia* and all negligence.[37]

76. The phials of perfume are said to be the prayers of the saints which are offered by the twenty-four ancients.[38]

77. These phials are to be understood as the love of God, or rather as the perfect and spiritual charity in which prayer is offered in spirit and in truth.

78. When you are of the mind that you do not stand in need of tears for your sins along with your prayer, then give some thought to the distance that separates you from God, whereas you ought to be in him constantly. Then you will shed more abundant tears than ever.

79. Surely when you take your own measure you will know a sweet sorrow and will call yourself, as Isaiah spoke of himself, a miserable wretch.[39] For you yourself are impure, your very lips are defiled and it is among such people as these rebels that you live and yet you dare to stand before the Lord of Armies.[40]

80. If you pray in all truth you will come upon a deep sense of confidence. Then the angels will walk with you and enlighten you concerning the meaning of created things.

81. Know that the holy angels urge us on to pray. They are present with us amid rejoicing as they pray for us. So if we are

---

37. Rev 8:3. Negligence is the source of the first sin and the fall. See Guillaumont, *op. cit.,* 37.

38. Rev 5:8.   39. Is 6:5.

40. With Hausherr this translation follows the text of the *Philokalia.* The Migne texts omits "among such people as these rebels."

careless and admit distracting thoughts we provoke them sharply inasmuch as they are joining in the fight on our behalf and we do not even take care to intercede with God on our own behalf. On the contrary by this contempt of their services and by this forsaking of their God and Ruler we fall in with the designs of the impure demons.

82. Pray with fitting reverence and without anxiety; sing with understanding and with attention to the requirements of the music —then you will soar aloft like young eagles.

83. The singing of Psalms quiets the passions and calms the intemperance of the body. Prayer, on the other hand, prepares the spirit to put its own powers into operation.

84. Prayer is activity which is appropriate to the dignity of the spirit; or better, it is appropriate for its nobler and adequate operation.[41]

85. Psalm-singing is an image of wisdom which is many-sided; prayer is the prelude to immaterial and uniform knowledge.[42]

86. Knowledge! The great possession of man. It is a fellow-worker with prayer, acting to awaken the power of thought to contemplate the divine knowledge.

87. If as yet you have not received the grace of prayer or of psalmody, then press ahead eagerly. You will gain hold of it.

88. In a parable the Lord spoke of the need for constant prayer

41. This reading follows Hausherr's suggestion which emends κρῆσις into χρῆσις ; *Leçons*, 117.

42. We have substituted ἀποικίλης for ποικίλης since the context obviously demands this meaning, that is to say it calls for "uniform" or "simple" knowledge, not multiform or varied knowledge as both Migne and the *Philokalia* have it. See Hausherr, *Leçons*, 119.

and of the avoidance of discouragement.[43] Do not fall into despondency if at times you do not get what you ask for. Keep up your courage. It will come later. For the Lord went on to tell another parable: "If I do not fear God and have no reverence for man, yet since this woman affords me such pains I had better do her justice."[44] The same thing will happen to those who cry out to God day and night—he will give them justice, and do it quickly. Take courage then, and persevere in your holy prayer with all sails unfurled.

89. Do not set your heart on what seems good to you but rather what is pleasing to God when you pray. This will free you from disturbance and leave you occupied with thanksgiving in your prayer.

90. Though you seem to be in God's presence, yet guard against the demon of unchastity. There is no more destructive or deceptive fellow than he. He would give the impression of being swifter than thought, and that he penetrates the watchfulness of your spirit. He would have you believe that your spirit is distracted from God when in fact it stands in his presence in fear and with reverence.

91. If you have a real interest in prayer then be prepared to withstand the assaults of the demon and endure with constancy the lashes he lays on. He shall attack you like a wild beast and buffet your entire body.

92. Train yourself like a skilled athlete. You must learn not to become anxious even if you should see some sudden apparition, or some sword pointed at you, or a beam of light leaping toward your face. Even though you should see some hideous and bloody figure, still stand firm, and in nowise give way to the fear that clutches at your heart. When you thus bear witness to your faith you will face your enemies with ready confidence.

---

43. Lk 18:1.   44. Lk 18:4-5.

93. The man who endures painful things will some day also find consoling ones. The man who is constant in disagreeable matters will not be without pleasant ones as well.

94. See to it that the evil demons do not lead you astray by means of some vision. Rather be wise: turn to prayer and call upon God to enlighten you if the thought comes from him, and if it does not, ask him to drive away from you the deceptive one quickly. Then take courage, for the dog will not hold his ground. With you praying to God with such ardor he shall be at once driven far off under the invisible lashings laid on by the unseen power of God.

95. It is proper that you be advised about another ruse. The demons divide up into two groups for a time, and when they see you calling out for help against the one group the others make their appearance under the form of angels who drive away the first group. They have in mind to deceive you into believing that they are holy angels in all truth.

96. Strive to cultivate a deep humility and the malice of the demons shall not touch your soul. Then the plague shall not approach your dwelling for "he has given his angels the command to watch over you"[45] and to drive away from you, invisibly, every hostile force.

97. Crashing sounds and roars and voices and beatings—all of these, coming from the devils, are heard by the man who pursues the practice of pure prayer. Yet he does not lose courage nor his presence of mind. He calls out to God: "I shall fear no evils for you are with me."[46] And he adds other similar prayers.

98. At the time of these temptations make use of short and intense prayer.

45. Ps 90:11.   46. Ps 22:4.

99. If the demons threaten you, appearing suddenly from the atmosphere and frightening you greatly and shattering your spirit or mauling your flesh like wild beasts, do not give way to panic because of them. Do not so much as trouble yourself over their threats. They frighten you so as to test your mettle. They wish to see if you will take them seriously or if you ignore them through contempt and whether you communicate in prayer with the omnipotent God, the Creator and Provider of all.

100. If it is before the omnipotent God, Creator and Provider of all, that you stand in your prayer, how is it that you foolishly ignore the fear of him which is beyond all measure, and you fear instead mosquitoes and roaches? Have you not heard Moses tell you: "The Lord your God shall you fear,"[47] or again: "Whom they dread and fear in the presence of his power . . .";[48]

101. Just as bread is nourishment for the body and virtue for the soul, so is spiritual prayer nourishment for the intelligence.

102. Pray not as the Pharisee but as the Publican in the holy place of prayer, so that you also may be justified by the Lord.

103. Strive to avoid praying against anyone in your prayer so that you do not destroy what you have been building up by making your prayer a defilement.

104. Learn a lesson from the man who owed ten thousand talents: unless you forgive the man who owes you a debt you yourself will not find forgiveness. For our Lord said: "He was given over to the hangman."[49]

105. Despise the needs of the body while you are engaged in prayer lest you do some damage to that unsurpassed gift that you gain by prayer due to the sting of some flea or even a louse, fly or mosquito.

47. Deut 6:13.   48. Ex 15:16.   49. Mt 18:24–35.

106. We once heard a story about one of the holy men of prayer who was assailed by the spiteful demon. No sooner had he lifted his hands in prayer than this demon transformed himself into a lion and, raising his forelegs up, he sunk his claws into either cheek of this athlete of prayer. But this man simply would not yield. He did not lower them until he had completed all his usual prayers.

107. We know that John the Short was a man of the same stamp —in fact it were more proper to refer to him as John the Greatest of Monks. He lived his solitary life in a ditch, and would remain unmoved in his communion with God even while the demon wrapped himself around him in the form of a great serpent that squeezed his flesh and vomited in his face.

108. Doubtless you have also heard of the monks of Tabennisi. It is related that, on one occasion when Abbot Theodore was speaking to the brethren, two vipers crawled up right between his feet. Well, he remained undisturbed and made a kind of arch of his feet to keep them there till he should finish his talk. Only then did he show them to the brethren and told them what had happened.

109. There was another spiritual man about whom we have read. While he was praying one day a viper crawled up to him and seized his foot. He did not so much as lower his arms until he finished his customary prayer, and he suffered no harm whatever from thus loving God above his own self.[50]

110. Keep your eyes lowered while you are praying. Deny your flesh and your desires and live according to the spirit.

50. This and the preceding chapters are curiously reminiscent of a passage in the Talmud dealing with prayer (*Tefillah*): "(when praying) even if a snake is wound round his heel he should not break off." *The Talmud,* "Barakoth," 5, ed., I. Epstein vol. 1 (London, 1961), 187. This is but another point of contact with a Jewish milieu that marks the writings of Evagrius. This area deserves further study.

111. There was another holy man living the solitary life in the desert. The demons pressed in upon him, surrounded him for a period of two weeks, tossing him up in the air and letting him fall on a mattress. Yet in no wise were they able to cause him to leave off his ardent prayer.

112. Two angels once came up to another man who was very dear to God—a man much given to prayer. Well, he was walking along in the desert at the time and they joined him in his journey, one on this side, another on that. For his part he gave them no attention lest he should detract in some way from "the better part," keeping in mind the admonition of the Apostle: "Neither angels nor principalities nor powers can separate us from the love of Christ."[51]

113. By true prayer a monk becomes another angel,[52] for he ardently longs to see the face of the Father in heaven.

114. Do not by any means strive to fashion some image or visualize some form at the time of prayer.

115. Do not cherish the desire to see sensibly angels or powers or even Christ lest you be led completely out of your wits, and taking a wolf for your shepherd, come to adore the demons who are your enemies.

116. Vainglory is the source of the illusions of your mind. When it exerts its influence on the mind it attempts to enclose the Divinity in form and figure.

51. Rom 8:35.

52. Lk 20:36 where the word used here by Evagrius, ἰσάγγελος, is found on the lips of our Lord himself. In Migne the second half of this sentence has slipped into the next one. Wagenaar, *op. cit.,* 524, gives reasons for translating here "another angel" rather than "the equal of an angel."

117. Let me repeat this saying of mine that I once expressed on some other occasions: Happy is the spirit that attains to perfect formlessness at the time of prayer.[53]

118. Happy is the spirit which, praying without distraction, goes on increasing its desire for God.

119. Happy is the spirit that becomes free of all matter and is stripped of all at the time of prayer.

120. Happy is the spirit that attains to complete unconsciousness of all sensible experience at the time of prayer.[54]

121. Happy is the man who thinks himself no better than dirt.

122. Happy is the monk who views the welfare and progress of all men with as much joy as if it were his own.

123. Happy is the monk who considers all men as god—after God.[55]

53. There is some doubt about the authentic Greek text of this brief chapter. We give the reading attested by Coislin Ms 109 and adopted by Hausherr. For the variant reading in Migne and a discussion of its significance, see *Leçons*, 150–54.

54. Literally the text reads: "Happy the spirit which attains to total insensibility at prayer." But translated this way in English it suggests the possibility that pure prayer is equal to sleep or a sheer black-out, which is far removed from Evagrius' thought. What he intends to convey is the concept of a prayer so pure and so rapt on its transcendent object that it absorbs the full being, consciousness and unconscious functioning as well. This teaching is explained in his Hellenistic system, yet it conveys the teaching of the desert, for St Anthony had taught, "That prayer is not perfect in the course of which the monk is aware of the fact that he is praying." Cassian, *Conferences* 9:31 (PL 49:808).

55. This deep respect for one's fellow man goes very far toward combating one of the chief accusations made against Desert spirituality, namely that it is egocentric. Growth in pure prayer leads to deepened regard for the dignity of one's fellow man. Theologically this idea is founded on the view of man as the image of God.

124. A monk is a man who is separated from all and who is in harmony with all.

125. A monk is a man who considers himself one with all men because he seems constantly to see himself in every man.[56]

126. Would you wish to know who is the man that prays perfectly? The one who brings forth all the best of thoughts for God.

127. Avoid every lie and all oaths since you desire to pray as a monk. Otherwise you are a vain pretender when you wear a habit, seeming to be something you are not.

128. If you desire to pray in the spirit then take nothing from the flesh so that you will not have some cloud darkening your vision at the time of prayer.

129. Trust in God for the needs of your body and then it will be clear that you are also relying upon him for the needs of your spirit.

130. If you attain to the (evangelical) promises you shall rule as a king. Keep your eye on this truth and you will count your present poverty a sweet thing.

131. Do not reject poverty and affliction. They are not trifling materials for the edifice of prayer.

132. Let the virtues that deal with the body be a pledge of the virtues of the soul, and those of the soul a pledge of those dealing with the spirit, and these latter a pledge of immaterial knowledge.

56. With Hausherr this translation follows the *Philokalia* text.

133. When you are praying against some evil thoughts and you find that you are freed from them readily, examine how this comes about lest you fall into some hidden trap, and by being deceived betray yourself.

134. It happens at times that the demons suggest some bad thoughts to you and again stir you up to pray against them, as is only proper, or to contradict them. Then they depart of their own choosing so as to deceive you into believing that you have conquered your thoughts of yourself and have cast fear into the demons.

135. If you pray against your passions or the demons that assail you[57] recall to mind the man who said: "I shall pursue after my enemies and shall lay hold of them and shall not turn aside until they all fall. I shall crush them and they shall not be able to stand. They shall fall beneath my feet . . . etc."[58] You are to say this at the appropriate moment thus arming yourself against your adversary with humility.

136. Do not think you have attained to virtue until first you have fought to the shedding of blood. One must resist sin even unto death—manfully and irreproachably, as the divine Apostle tells us.[59]

137. If you do good to some one or other, be sure of it, another man comes along and does you an ill turn. This is calculated to make you yield under the pressure of injustice and do something injurious to another. In this way you would miserably scatter what you had so well gathered up—and precisely this is the aim of the demons. So be on your guard.

138. Keep an eye out for the grievous assaults of the devil; give thought to a way of putting an end to your servitude to him.

---

57. We follow the *Philokalia* here as Hausherr recommends.
58. Ps 17:38–39.
59. Heb 12:4.

139. By night the demons demand the spiritual master for themselves—to harass him. By day they surround him with pressures from men—with calumnies and with dangers.

140. Do not seek to avoid those who would give you a good drubbing. Though they kick you about and stretch you and hackle you like flax, yet after all this is the way the fuller cleans your clothes.[60]

141. Inasmuch as you have not renounced the passions but resist virtue and truth with your spirit, you will not find fragrant perfume in your bosom.

142. Do you wish to pray? Then banish the things of this world. Have heaven for your homeland and live there constantly—not in mere word but in actions that imitate the angels and in a more god-like knowledge.

143. If you remember the Judge only when you are in difficulties as One who inspires fear and who is incorruptibly honest, then you have not as yet learned to "serve the Lord in fear and to rejoice in him with trembling."[61] For understand this point well: one is to worship him even in spiritual relaxations and in times of good cheer with even more piety and reverence.

144. A wise man is one who does not cease to recall the painful memory of his own sins before he has been perfectly converted—and the eternal punishment by fire that they merit as well.

145. A man who is still held by sin and still subject to fits of anger and yet dares shamelessly to strive after knowledge of more divine things or to rise up to the level of immaterial prayer is to be rebuked

60. Correcting αἴσθησις of Migne to ἐσθής of the *Philokalia*, see Hausherr, *Leçons*, 172.

61. Ps 2:11.

in the words of the Apostle where he gives it out that not with impunity does he pray with his head bare[62] and uncovered. "Such a soul is to have domination over its head because of the holy angels who are present," St Paul tells us,[63] that is to say, it is to be covered by respect and fitting humility.

146. Just as it hardly is of benefit to a man with bad eyes to stand gazing at the midday sun, when it is hottest, with fixed attention and uncovered[64] eyes, so also is it of no avail at all for an impure spirit, still subject to passions, to counterfeit that awesome and surpassing prayer in spirit and truth. On the contrary, it stirs up the resentment of God against itself.

147. If he who has need of nothing and who is not liable to be corrupted by any bribe does not receive the gift of a man who draws near to the altar before that man reconciles himself with his neighbor who has some grief against him, then consider what great circumspection and prudence we need if we are to offer incense that is well-pleasing to God on the spiritual altar.

148. Do not find your joy in words of praise if you do not want sinners to cut you up no longer on the back but on your face.[65] Then too you will be mocked at by them at the time of prayer as you are drawn away, allured by them with monstrous thoughts.

149. When attention seeks prayer it finds it. For if there is anything that marches in the train of attention it is prayer; and so it must be cultivated.

150. Just as sight is the most worthy of the senses, so also is prayer the most divine of the virtues.

62. Read ἀκατακάλυπτος, not ἀκάλυπτος of Migne. Cf. Hausherr, *Leçons*, 176.
63. 1 Cor 11:10.
64. We have adopted, with Hausherr, the *Philokalia* reading of ἀκατακάλυπτος for ἀκατάλυπτος of Migne.
65. Cf. Ps 128:3.

151. The value of prayer is found not merely in its quantity but also in its quality. This is made clear by those two men who entered the temple, and also by this saying: "When you pray do not do a lot of empty chattering . . ."[66]

152. To the extent that you still give attention to the values of the body, and your mind concerns itself with the amenities of life, you have not yet seen the place of prayer. Rather the happiness of this way is still far off.

153. When you give yourself to prayer, rise above every other joy—then you will find true prayer.

---

66. Lk 18:10 and Mt 6:7.

I am grateful to T. C. Lawlor for his helpful suggestions which led to certain improvements in the text.

The Editors would also like to express their gratitude to G. Smerillo, Pembroke College, Oxford, for his assistance in preparing this volume for publication.

SELECTED BIBLIOGRAPHY

Altaner, B., *Patrology*. Trans. H. Graef (New York, 1960).

Bardenhewer, O., *Geschichte der altkirchlichen Literatur*, vol. 3 (Freiburg, 1923).

Beck, H. G., *Kirche und Theologische Literatur im Byzantinischen Reich* (Munich, 1959).

Bousset, W., *Apophthegmata: Studien zur Geschichte des altesten Mönchtums* (Tübingen, 1922).

Bouyer, L., *The Spirituality of the New Testament and the Fathers* (New York, 1963).

Budge, E. A. W., *The Book of Paradise: Being the Histories and Sayings of the Monks and Ascetics of the Egyptian Desert*. 2 vols. (London, 1904).

Butler, C., *The Lausiac History of Palladius*. 2 vols. (Cambridge, 1898, 1904).

Chadwick, O., *John Cassian: A study in Primitive Monasticism* (Cambridge, 2 ed., 1967).

Frankenberg, W., *Evagrios Pontikus* (Berlin, 1912).

Guillaumont, A., *Les "Kephalaia Gnostica" d'Evagre le Pontique* (Paris, 1962).

——*Les Six Centuries des "Kephalaia Gnostica" d'Evagre le Pontique*. PO, 28:1 (Paris, 1958).

Guillaumont, A. and C., *Traité Pratique ou le Moine*, SC 170, 171 (Paris, 1971).

Hausherr, I., "Le 'De Oratione' d'Evagre le Pontique en Syriaque et en Arabe," OCP, 5 (1939), 7–77.

——"Les grands courants de la spiritualité orientale," OCP, 1 (1935), 114–138.

——*Les Lecons d'un Contemplative: Le Traité de l'Oraison d'Evagre le Pontique* (Paris, 1960).

Le Maître, J., Roques, R., Viller, M., "Contemplation chez les Grecs et autres orientaux chrétiennes," DS, 2:1762–1787 (1950–1952).

Lorié, L. T. A., *Spiritual Terminology in the Latin Translations of the "Vita Antonii"* (Nijmegen, 1955).

Marsili, S., *Giovanni Cassiano ed Evagrio Pontica. Studia Anselmiana* 5 (Rome, 1936).

Muyldermans, J., *Evagrian Syriaca: Textes indiéts du British Museum et de la Vaticane. Bibliothéque Muséon,* 31 (Louvain, 1952).

Nikodemus the Hagiorite, Macarius of Corinth, *Philokalia.* 6 vols. 3 ed. (Athens, 1957–1963).

Ortiz de Urbina, I., *Patrologia Syriaca.* 2 ed. (Rome, 1965).

Palladius, *The Lausiac History.* Trans. R. T. Meyer. *Ancient Christian Writers* 34 (Washington, 1964).

Quasten, J., *Patrology.* 3 vols (Westminster, Md., 1950–1960).

Viller, M., "Aux Sources de la Spiritualité de S. Maxime: Les Oeuvres d'Evagre le Pontique," RAM, 11 (1930), 156–184, 239–268.

Völker, W., *Maximus Confessor als Meister des geistlichen Lebens* (Weisbaden, 1965).

Von Ivánka, E., *Plato Christianus* (Einsiedeln, 1964).

OLD AND NEW TESTAMENT

*Vulgate enumeration.

M

GENERAL INDEX

abandonment, 61.
abba, xlv.
abstinence, 17.
acedia, lxvii, lxviii, 17, 18, 22, 23, 24, 25, 26, 68.
Ad gentes, ix.
affectivity, lxvii, 36, 37.
affliction, 76.
agape, lxxxii, lxxxiii, lxxxiv, 14, 25, 36.
Alexandria, xxiii, xxix, xli, xliii, xliv, xlvi, lxvii, 40.
Alexandrians, lxxxviii.
allegory, lxxi.
almsgiving, 20, 21.
altar, 58, 79.
anachoresis, 30.
Ancyra, xxxii.
angel, lxxvi, lxxvii, lxxviii, lxxx, 6, 23, 31, 36, 38, 41, 59, 61, 67, 71, 74, 78, 79.
angelic. lxxviii, lxxix, 61.
anger, lxxvi, 17, 18, 20, 21, 22, 23, 25, 26, 27, 35, 36, 58, 59, 62, 63, 65, 78.
angry, 22, 41, 57, 59.
Anima, De, xvii.
Annesi, xxxvi.
anthropological, lx.
anthropology, xvii.
anthropomorphic, xlviii.
Antipelagians, lxxxvii.
Antirrheticos, xii, lxii, lxxxi, 12, 22, 28.
anxiety, 33, 69.
anxious, 60, 70.
apatheia, xlvii, lxviii, lxxii, lxxiii, lxxxii, -lxxxviii, 4, 14, 19, 25, 31-34, 36, 46, 49, 51, 63.

apex mentis, xvii.
aphorisms, lxvii.
Apocalypse, 68.
Apollinarianism, xliv.
Apophthegmata, liv, lxxxi.
approval, 61.
Aquileia, xxvii.
Arabic, 1.
archdeacon, xxxvii, xxxviii.
archetype, xcii.
Arianism, xxxvii, xliv.
Arians, lxviii.
Armenia, 1.
Armenian, xxvi, xxx, li, lviii, lx, lxi-lxv.
arrogance, xliv, 59.
Ascension of Isaias, lxxx.
ascent, 60.
ascesis, lxxvii, 3, 4, 36, 47.
ascetic, lxxi, lxxx, lxxxi, lxxxiii, lxxxiv, 6, 14, 17, 19, 25, 33, 34, 36, 37, 41, 55.
ascetical: see theology.
Assyria, 13.
Athos, lvi.
attention, 69, 74, 79, 80.
attentive, 23.
attitudes, 31.
avarice, 14, 17, 25, 63.
avenge, 57, 62.
awareness, 34.
awkwardness, 24.

banquets, 31.
beasts, 18, 21, 31, 41, 70.
beatitude, lxxxi, 14.
belt, 14.
Benedictine, xiii, xiv, xvi, lii, liii, 46.

CISTERCIAN FATHERS SERIES

Under the direction of the same Board of Editors as the *Cistercian Studies Series*, the *Cistercian Fathers Series* seeks to make available the works of the Cistercian Fathers in good English translations based on the recently established critical editions. The texts are accompanied by introductions, notes and indexes prepared by qualified scholars.